TAXATION S
March Bu

For a complete list of Management Books 2000 titles,
visit our web-site on http://www.mb2000.com

TAXATION SIMPLIFIED
March Budget 2005

Editor: James Alexander
in association with Richard Somers FCA
and Tony Jones BA ATT

100th EDITION

2000

First published in 2005 by Management Books 2000 Ltd
Forge House, Limes Road
Kemble, Cirencester
Gloucestershire, GL7 6AD, UK
Tel: 0044 (0) 1285 771441
Fax: 0044 (0) 1285 771055
E-mail: info@mb2000.com
Web: www.mb2000.com

Printed and bound in Great Britain by Digital Books Logistics of Peterborough

British Library Cataloguing in Publication Data is available
ISBN 1-85252-492-8

Contents

CHAPTER 4 – BUSINESS TAXATION

CHAPTER 5 – CAPITAL GAINS

CHAPTER 6 – RENTS FROM PROPERTY

CHAPTER 7 – MISCELLANEOUS MATTERS

PREFACE TO THE 100th EDITION

Oh yes, this is the 100th Edition - and we are quite proud of that fact. Mind you, we at MB2000 would be very hard pressed to lay our hands on the very early editions! We acquired the title many years ago after a long and distinguished career, and have remodelled and revamped it several times since then. This style has been the pattern since 1996 and the oldest edition on our archive shelves dates from 1993. That was a physically smaller book with a very small typeface.

This edition is based on the March 2005 Budget, which was somewhat overshadowed by the promise of an impending General Election some few weeks later. The papers' headlines on the day after the Budget reflected this feeling - 'It's the rob you later budget' (Daily Express); 'Beware the Bribes of March!' (The Sun); 'A Manifesto, not a Budget' (The Times). The inner headlines also showed that Gordon Brown was not everyone's best friend. Vote now, pay later; Brown bribe for the grey vote; Middle Britain will pay through the nose - although the general opinion was that most people will be fractionally better off. Certainly there were some pleasing gifts to the older members of the population, with some relief on council tax and free bus passes, but the changes in the main were seen by many commentators as pre-election flannel with a certainty of later tax increases, despite protestations to the contrary by the Chancellor.

First time home buyers were encouraged by the raising of the threshold for payment of stamp duty, although this was more advantageous in some regions than others. Families with children will benefit from further tax credits although those families at the top and the bottom of the earnings league will barely see any differences at all.

Pensioners will see some benefits this year, with increases in winter fuel payments for the over-80s, free local bus travel for over-60s and contributions towards the cost of council tax for people over 65. All this was greeted with some scepticism by politicians and carers alike, claiming that it was merely a bribe and that these measures didn't really meet the needs of pensioners. The probability is that, no matter what any Chancellor proposes, there will be critics and pooh-poohers.

The Budget did however promise several billions more spending on transport, education, defence and health. But wouldn't any Chancellor have done that a few weeks before a General Election? As we mentioned earlier, there was a general feeling that much of the detail emanating from the Budget speech was devised largely to help secure a third term for Tony Blair and his Government. What would have happened if the Tories or the LibDems had won is anybody's guess - we will never know.

James Alexander, Richard Somers, Tony Jones, Gloucestershire, May 2005

SUMMARY OF RATES AND ALLOWANCES

A. RATES OF TAX

1. Income Tax (Net income after allowances) – non-savings income

2004/05		2005/06	
first £2,020	10%	first £2,090	10%
£2,021 to £31,400	22%	£2,091 to £32,400	22%
above £31,400	40%	above £32,400	40%

(see page 15 for details of the rates of tax payable on savings income)

2. Corporation Tax

	2004/05	2005/06
Starting Rate*		
£1 – £10,000	0%	0%
Intermediate Profits		
£10,001 – £50,000	23.75%	23.75%
Small Company Rate		
£50,001 – £300,000	19%	19%
Intermediate Profits		
£300,001 – £1 500,000	32.75%	32.75%
Large Company Rate		
£1,500,000+	30%	30%
* Small company distributed profits		
minimum rate	19%	19%
Small companies marginal		
relief fraction: 10,000-50,000	19/400	19/400
300,000-1,500,000	11/400	11/400

3. Capital Gains Tax

	2004/05	2005/06
(a) Individuals		
At marginal income tax rate		
(i.e. 10%, 20%, or 40%)		
Exemption limits:	£8,200	£8,500
(b) Companies		
At the corporation tax rate		
(c) Trusts		
Interest in possession trusts	40%	40%
Discretionary and A&M trusts	40%	40%
Exemption limits	£4,100	£4,250

4. Value Added Tax

	from 31.3.04	from 1.4.05
Registration limit	£58,000	£60,000
Deregistration limit	£56,000	£58,000

5. Inheritance Tax

	2004/05	2005/06
Zero band limit	£263,000	£275,000
Excess charged at	40%	40%

B. PERSONAL ALLOWANCES

	2004/05 £	2005/06 £
Personal allowance (each individual under 65)	4,745	4,895
Blind person's allowance	1,560	1,610
Age allowances:		
(a) Age 65-74		
Personal allowance	6,830	7.090
Married couple's allowance*	5,725	5,905
(b) Age 75 and over		
Personal allowance	6,950	7,220
Married couple's allowance*	5,795	5,975
Income limit for age allowances †	18,900	19,500

* Restricted to 10%

† If income exceeds this, then the age allowances are reduced by 50% of the excess down to the minimum amount. In the case of personal allowances, down to the under-65 amount. In the case of married couple's allowance, down to £2,280 (2004/05 £2,210).

TAX CREDITS

Working Tax Credit (WTC)

	2004/05 £	2005/06 £
Annual		
Basic element	1,570	1,620
Second adult or lone parent addition	1,545	1,595
30 hour element	640	660
Disability element	2,100	2,165
Severe disability element	890	920
Age 50+ element working 16-29 hours per week*	1.075	1,110
Age 50+ element working 30+ hours per week*	1,610	1,660
Weekly		
Childcare element		
- maximum eligible cost for 1 child	135	175
- maximum eligible cost for 2 or more children†	200	300

Claimants can be eligible for each element
Claim reduced by 37p for every £1 of annual income over £5,220

Mutually exclusive
†Reduced to 70% of eligible cost

Child Tax Credit (CTC)

	2004/05 £	2005/06 £
Annual		
Family element (double in year of birth)*	545	545
Child element (per child)†		
- disabled child	3,840	3,975
- severely disabled child	4,730	4,895
- any other child	1,625	1,690

* Claim reduced by £1 for every £15 of annual income over £50,000
† Where only CTC available, claim reduced by 37p for every £1 of annual income over £13,910 (£13,480 in 2004/05); £5,000 where CTC also available

Editorial note

As we stated last year, much of this year's book uses the same text as in previous editions, but that is because much of the basic material and explanations remains unchanged over the year. There might be an expectation that masses of stuff would change, but in reality, the business of making tax rules and laws is not one usually given to great upheaval. The changes tend to be in the details and the figures rather than in the overall concepts.

This book has all the changes announced by the Chancellor in his 16 March 2005 Budget, in a format that makes for easy reference. There is, therefore, a great deal of useful and focused detail that will help you meet your tax obligations and assist in solving your queries and problems. The book grows in repute and I am very pleased to be able to take the text and re-read and revise it year on year. I know that Richard and Tony also enjoy the challenge of taking the Government's pronouncements and trying to make readable sense of them.

Once again, we are pleased to find that the book is being used by some colleges as a set text. This is very encouraging and shows how the simplicity and ease of use is recognised by academics as well as by practitioners and taxpayers themselves.

If, as financial advisers and practitioners, or just enthusiastic amateurs, you would like to see any changes to our presentation, then do get in touch. An annual publication is a growing and shifting thing, and feedback from readers is one sure way of finding out where the book should be heading in the future. Thank you for your continued support.

It is pleasing to note that last year we received no comments from readers about possible errors or omissions, merely a few questions on matters of fact, which, between the three of us, we were able to answer.

You may not know that we already have a substantial subscription list for this publication. This allows regular purchasers to receive the book at a discount - and post free. It also means that the subscribers will receive their copies as soon as the book is published, without having to visit the bookshop to find it. If you would like to join this growing band, there is an application form at the back of the book.

JNA

1

The Tax System

As citizens, we should be able to discuss and, if necessary, criticise the government's measures for controlling the economy, in which taxation is an important factor, but we cannot sensibly do so without at least a basic understanding of the system. A more direct reason is that we are all entitled to arrange our affairs so that our personal tax liabilities are reduced to the legal minimum, and this, too, requires knowledge. Of equal importance is that we need to know how to avoid getting into financial difficulties in meeting the tax we are due to pay.

Many people are paying more tax than they need. This is not normally the fault of the tax offices, although mistakes do occur, and in simple cases, the situation can be easily remedied by the individual concerned. In more complicated cases it is desirable to obtain expert advice, but it is necessary to know when to seek that advice.

1.2 WHY TAXES ARE NECESSARY

The purposes for which taxation is required may be summarised as follows.

- Taxation is needed to pay for national expenditure on, for example, defence, government administration and interest on government borrowings – and in years like this one, on extensive military activity abroad; and for local expenditure such as for local services, health, education, welfare and interest on loans. National expenditure is met from taxes such as income tax, corporation tax, capital gains tax, and from customs and excise duties, such as value added tax, stamp duties and licence duties. Local expenditure is met from the rates, the council tax, and from grants from central government.

- Taxation is needed to enforce government financial policy, such as in controlling inflation and encouraging investment in industry.

The tax system is undoubtedly influenced by political motives, both in the wide and narrow sense. While we all naturally resent paying to the tax collector part of our hard-earned income, and feel that the burden on us individually is excessive, a principle of taxation is that it should be equitable as between one person and another. Everyone is, of course, entitled to their opinion as to the fairness of the system, but that opinion should be justified by knowledge.

1.3 LIABILITY TO TAX

All individuals resident in the United Kingdom of Great Britain and Northern Ireland are liable to pay income tax, capital gains tax and inheritance tax. Persons resident outside the UK, so far as they derive income from UK sources, are also liable to pay UK tax whether they are British subjects or not. Persons resident in the UK and receiving income from abroad are, in general, liable to UK tax on their overseas earnings, subject to certain reliefs and allowances. Companies are liable for corporation tax on income wherever it arises.

1.4 TAX RETURNS

All persons liable to UK taxation have the duty to complete Tax Returns and to submit them to the appropriate Inspector of Taxes. The form for a particular tax year shows the income received (including capital gains) and the applicable charges against income, for the previous tax year, as well as the allowances claimed for the current tax year. Inspectors of Taxes normally send out Self-assessment Tax Return forms early in each tax year, but they may not do so where all a taxpayer's income is covered by deduction of tax at source such as under the PAYE system for salaries and wages. (See 2.2 Self-Assessment). The 2004/05 tax return will have to be submitted to the Inland Revenue by 30.9.2005 if you wish the Inland Revenue to calculate your tax liability or by 31.1.06 if you calculate it yourself. Late submission will lead to an initial penalty of up to £100.

It is especially necessary to submit a Return to obtain all available tax allowances; to record investment income from shares, deposits and loans; to record sales and purchases of investments and other assets for capital gains; charges on income, such as mortgages and covenants, etc.; and where liability to higher rate tax may apply. It is particularly necessary to show untaxed income on the Return: for instance, interest not subject to deduction of tax at source, such as on many national savings and certain government securities. For individuals with small incomes, the submission of a full return may result in a refund of excess tax suffered by deduction from income. Failure to make a Return, or the submission of a false or incorrect Return, does involve interest and penalties.

1.5 SERVICES FROM THE INLAND REVENUE

Information and advice on tax is available from numerous Tax Enquiry Centres, including Mobile Centres, but the Inland Revenue is not obliged to advise on how tax can be reduced and certainly not on how it can be evaded. A wide range of leaflets is available from Tax Offices. Complaints may be made to an Adjudicator with regard to the manner in which the Inland Revenue has acted, but not on technical matters.

1.6 MINIMISING YOUR TAX

For the purpose of reducing your tax to the minimum legally payable, you should ask yourself the following questions:

● **Are you obtaining all the allowances to which you are entitled?** – See Chapter 2, *Personal Taxation*. If not, you may have failed to make the necessary returns to the Inspector of Taxes.

● **Do you have a balance of income, after deducting allowances and charges, on which tax is payable?** If not, you can reclaim from the Inland Revenue any excess tax deducted from interest, pensions, etc. Many married women, widows, divorcees, retired people and others with low income are liable for little if any tax and could recover some or all of the tax deducted at source from their income.

● **If you are in business, even as a spare time venture, are you charging all allowable expenses in your business accounts?** (See Chapter 4, *Tax on Business*.) Allowable expenses may include, for example, the business use of a car or reasonable fees or salaries paid to spouses or other relatives who assist in the business. Of particular importance are claims for capital allowances and the selection of starting dates.

● **Have you arranged your financial affairs so as to reduce your tax liabilities?** These arrangements could include, for instance, transfers of investments between husband and wife; life-time gifts to reduce inheritance tax; obtaining exemptions from capital gains tax; taking advantage of personal pensions and various tax-free investments. Reference should be made to the relevant chapters and sections of this book.

In this context, we cannot over-emphasise the dangers of attempting to evade tax by, for example, deliberately omitting to declare income or falsifying the figures. Even many expertly drawn schemes of tax avoidance have turned out to be ineffective or are eventually overtaken by legislation. The penalties, both personal and monetary, can be severe, and the tax authorities have many sources of information.

In a complicated situation, expert advice from a qualified accountant or solicitor specialising in the subject is necessary. The taxpayer should be wary of unqualified advisers or lounge-bar boasting! A great deal of help can be obtained from tax offices but it is not part of the duty of the officials to advise on tax minimisation.

In the more straightforward situations, the information contained in the following pages will be sufficient for the taxpayer to manage his or her own tax affairs; it will also show when specialist advice is needed.

1.7 PROVIDING FOR PAYMENT

Most of the **income tax** due is collected by deduction from income. One example of this is the system for deducting tax from wages and salaries known as the Pay As You Earn system (PAYE). Under this system the amount of tax deducted is controlled by a code which is notified to the employer. If the code has been correctly allocated, the amount of tax deducted will equal the amount due from the employee during the year. Another example is the deduction of tax at source from investment income such as interest. In this case the tax is deducted at a flat rate regardless of the person's tax liability.

Where income is received without being taxed at source, the tax due will generally be payable on 31 January in the year of assessment. However, where the tax is due on the profits of an individual's business there are three payment dates: 31 January in the tax year, and 31 July and 31 January following the tax year. The first two are payments on account, with a balancing payment (if any) on the 31 January immediately following the tax year concerned. The first two payments (on account) are estimates of the liability based on the actual liability of the previous tax year.

Obviously, if profits are rising, the payments on account will not cover the total liability and will therefore leave a sum due for the balancing payment. If profits are falling you can apply to reduce the payments on account. Interest is payable if it subsequently turns out that you reduced these by too much.

Where tax has been deducted from investment income, there will be a further liability to tax if the individual is liable to tax at the higher rate. In that case the tax will be payable on 31 January in the tax year following the tax year in which the income was received. (A tax year runs from 6 April to the following 5 April.)

Capital gains tax will also be payable on 31 January following the tax year in which the gain arose.

Companies are charged to **corporation tax** on all taxable income and gains. The assessment is based on the accounting period, and the tax is payable nine months after the end of that period.

Where tax is not paid on time, the Collector of Taxes will issue demands, and will charge interest on tax paid late.

It is important to avoid financial difficulties when large demands for tax are received. This applies, in particular, to business profits, higher-rate income tax, and tax on untaxed interest. The remedy is to provide for the tax in advance through regular savings out of current income, but for that purpose it is necessary to know when the tax will become due and to be able to forecast the amount.

In too many cases, people fail to make returns to the Inspector of Taxes, or make incorrect returns, of the income they receive. This particularly applies to occasional work and spare-time activities. This may be due to ignorance of the tax regulations or genuine mistakes, but the almost inevitable consequence is that tax demands on the undeclared income are received going back for six years, or longer where there is fraud. In the latter case, severe penalties may be charged in addition to the tax due. Delay in payment will give rise to interest being charged in addition.

In 2005, the last date to notify the Inland Revenue of chargeability to tax for 2004/05 is 5 October 2005. Failure to do so will lead to a penalty of up to 100% of any tax paid late. The newly self-employed have to notify the Inland Revenue of starting to trade within 3 months of the end of the month in which they started – e.g. Brown starts his business on 1 May 2005 and he has until 30 August 2005 to notify. Otherwise, a penalty of £100 is due.

The self-assessment tax return will be issued in April 2005. Details of the accounts period ending in 2004/05 should be entered thereon. A sum of tax, based on the 2003/04 actual liability will already have been paid by 31 January 2005, and a similar sum is due on 31 July 2005. The tax return itself need not be returned to the Inland Revenue until 31 January 2006. On this date, the balance of any tax due must be paid. This date should be kept to in order to avoid penalties and interest.

Collectors will not hesitate to take legal action to obtain long overdue tax. They may sue in the Courts, and distrain on the taxpayer's furniture and effects. Many people have been made bankrupt and companies liquidated for unpaid tax.

Certificates of Tax Deposit may be obtained to provide for the potential liability for income tax which is in dispute, thus avoiding an interest charge.

1.8 THE ADMINISTRATION OF THE SYSTEM

How taxation is authorised

The statutory authority for the imposition of taxation is contained in the following Acts of Parliament:

- Income and Corporation Taxes Act 1988 (a Consolidating Act).
- The Taxes Management Act 1970, covering the administration of taxation.
- The Provisional Collection of Taxes Act 1968, permitting the Budget proposals to be enforced until amended.
- The Capital Allowances Act 2001, providing for allowances on the acquisition of fixed assets by business instead of depreciation.
- Taxation of Chargeable Gains Act 1992.
- Value Added Tax Act 1994.
- Inheritance Tax Act 1984.
- Income Tax (Earnings and Pensions) Act 2003.

This legislation is amended by the annual (usually July) and sometimes more frequent Finance Acts.

This enormous volume of legislation has to be interpreted by the Courts in an even greater volume of decided cases. In addition, the Inland Revenue from time to time publish 'concessions and practice notes', where the strict application of the law would be unjust or unworkable, and to indicate the methods they employ in particular situations.

Proposed amendments and additions to the current law and practice of taxation are presented to Parliament by the Chancellor of the Exchequer by way of a pre-Budget speech in December, and in his Budget Speech, usually in March of each year. Occasionally, especially in an election year, there may be more than one Budget. Had there been a change of Government on 5 May this year, you can be certain that there would have been a second Budget! The 'Budget' is strictly a forecast of government income and expenditure for the coming year, and includes a review of the previous year's results.

The Budget proposals are set out in the Finance Bill which is then debated in Parliament. The provisions of the Finance Bill have immediate effect under the Provisional Collection of Taxes Act. Amendments made during the debate are incorporated in the Finance Act of the following July which may entail adjustments to the taxation provisionally imposed.

Historical note

If you are puzzled or frustrated by having to pay income tax, bear in mind that it has been in existence in the UK since William Pitt the Younger introduced income tax to help fund the Napoleonic Wars, in 1799. The rate was 10% on anyone who earned more than £60 per year. How times change! After the Battle of Waterloo in 1816, income tax was repealed and all the records were burned as people believed that such taxes should only be levied to finance wars. However, copies were retained by the King's Remembrancer (nice title). I dare say there are a few people nowadays who would be pleased to see all tax records burned, but there is not much chance of that.

Probably the best known tax story is that of Lady Godiva, whose husband, Leofric, Earl of Mercia, promised to reduce the amount of tax he imposed on the people of Coventry if she rode naked through the streets of the town - a fine legend and one which also gave rise to the story of Peeping Tom, no doubt a taxpayer as well.

Taxes have been levied since ancient times, by good and bad leaders - and for some strange reasons. During the reigns of the Pharaohs in ancient Egypt, a tax was raised on cooking oil and tax scribes would audit households to see that people were not cooking in left-over oils from other processes. In colonial America, tax was paid on sugar and molasses. Ancient Athenians imposed a monthly poll tax on foreigners - is there a hint here of further possible revenue for the UK? Julius Caesar imposed a 1% sales tax and in Caesar Augustus' time, there was a 4% sales tax on slaves. In more recent times, some American states have levied odd taxes such as one on visiting entertainers and athletes, or on packs of playing cards with less than 54 cards. That meant that you needed an extra joker or a trip to the neighbouring State. Taxes have also been levied on jockeys, windows and fireplaces.

As a final historical thought, in the light of current political manoeuvring for power, the following people were all Chancellors of the Exchequer before becoming Prime Minister - Addington, Pitt, Disraeli, Gladstone, Lloyd George, Baldwin, Chamberlain, Churchill, Macmillan, Callaghan, Major - who next?

The fiscal year and the assessment year

The government accounting year for taxation purposes, or the 'fiscal year', ends on 5 April, and income tax assessments are made for each year ending on that date. There is a slight difference in the assessment year for corporation tax on limited companies and other corporate bodies and in these cases the 'financial year' ends on 31 March, thus conforming to the standard 'reference year' for such bodies under the Companies Acts.

For most of an individual's income – for example, income from employment – tax is calculated on the actual amount received in the year of assessment, at the rates of tax applicable to that year. For some income, notably the profits of a partnership or business in single ownership, the assessment year will normally cover the income shown by the accounts made up to a date in the year of assessment.

Corporate bodies, including limited companies, are charged to corporation tax on the taxable profits shown by their accounts for their accounting years. The rate of corporation tax applied is the rate applicable to the tax years covered by the accounting period. This is payable 9 months after the year end.

Organisation of the Inland Revenue

The general administration of the taxation system is the responsibility of the Board of the Inland Revenue, of which the members are called the 'Commissioners of Taxes'. Under the Board are (a) Inspectors of Taxes and (b) Collectors of Taxes. Inspectors have offices in tax districts which roughly correspond to the local authority areas but in some cases an Inspectorate is centralised to deal with a particular class of taxpayer, e.g. civil servants. Tax offices dealing with employments in London have been moved to provincial towns. Tax collection accounting has been computerised in Cumbernauld and Shipley.

Widespread reorganisation of Tax Offices began in January 1993. In many areas Taxpayer Service Offices combine the collection of tax with all but specialist work on assessments, personal reliefs and PAYE coding. Most taxpayers will, as a result, be saved the trouble of dealing with a number of tax offices. District Offices will be responsible for compliance with tax rules, audit functions and examining business accounts. Taxpayer Assistance Offices will assist the taxpayer in enquiries.

The Inspectors have the responsibility of examining taxpayers' Returns of Income, issuing codes under PAYE, dealing with appeals, negotiating adjustments, and authorising repayments of tax. They have wide powers to require the production of documents and Inspectors can apply to a magistrate for the right to enter a taxpayer's premises.

The Collectors are in effect the cashiers of the Inland Revenue. They have the responsibility of ensuring collection from the taxpayer of the tax due under the assessment. They have no power to alter the assessment but they may in suitable cases agree to receive payment by instalments. If a taxpayer is finding difficulty in meeting his tax liability he or she would be well advised to discuss the problem with the Collector promptly and make a reasonable arrangement for payment. As with many things in life, if the taxpayer is up front, the collector is more likely to be flexible.

The General Commissioners of Taxes are persons of local repute, akin to magistrates, and not responsible to the Inland Revenue. Their function is to hear appeals by the taxpayer from the decision of the Inspector and to protect the interests of the taxpayer, subject to law. Alternatively, the taxpayer can appeal against a decision of the Inspector to the Special Commissioners. The latter are appointed by the Lord Chancellor and are experts in taxation law and practice. The General Commissioners are best qualified to deal with questions of local circumstances.

In May 1993 an independent Adjudicator was appointed to consider complaints from taxpayers, but will not deal with questions of law or valuations.

Money laundering

Any new clients who approach any firm, be they accountants, lawyers, banks, estate agents or whatever, have to provide personal details such as passport, driving licence and current utilities bill, in order to prove that they are who they say they are. Photocopies of these documents must be filed as evidence that checks have been made. Failure to do so will render the adviser firm liable to prosecution. Similar threats of possible liability for advisers now exist if that adviser is party to knowledge of error or fraud, however innocent, and it is not reported to NCIS (National Criminal Intelligence Service).

1.9 THE CATEGORIES OF TAX

Probably no one escapes the tax net in some form or another. We all suffer value added tax (VAT) on many purchases; most of us pay income tax, the council tax and National Insurance contributions; many are liable for capital gains tax. Companies pay corporation tax, capital gains tax, excise duties, VAT and business rates. For a full understanding of the system it is therefore desirable to consider all the taxes in which we may be involved.

Taxes are usually described as either direct or indirect and this classification is used below, although the distinction between the two categories is not always precise. Direct taxes are those charged directly on individuals, partnerships, trusts and corporate bodies and indirect taxes are of more general application.

(a) Direct taxes

Income tax. Charged on the total income of individuals, including their salaries, wages, pensions, fees and other remuneration; their dividends, interest and royalties; profits from business they operate alone or in partnership; and many other kinds of income, including for example, certain National Insurance benefits, alimony, etc. The rate of tax payable depends on the type of income. A distinction must be made between non-savings income, dividends and other savings income.

For non-savings income, the income tax rates on taxable income are as follows:

	2004/05		2005/06	
	Band	Rate	Band	Rate
	£	%	£	%
Starting	0-2,020	10%	0-2,090	10%
Basic	2,021 - 31,400	22%	2,091-32,400	22%
Higher	over 31,400	40%	over 32,400	40%

In the case of most savings income other than dividends, tax is deducted at the lower rate of 20%. Taxpayers with taxable income below the basic rate limit have no further tax to pay. Those with income above the basic rate limit have to pay a further 20%.

UK dividends are paid net of a tax credit of 10% of the gross dividend. Basic rate taxpayers have no further tax to pay, but higher rate taxpayers have a further liability of 22½%.

Corporation tax. Payable by limited companies and other corporate bodies on their profits, at 30% for large companies and 19% for small companies. For the year to 31 March 2006, there is a starting rate of 0% on the first £10,000 increasing on a sliding scale to 19% at £50,000.

The Government has been concerned at the amounts of tax revenue it has lost through tax mitigation strategies based on incorporation and the subsequent extraction of profits via dividends. So, for distributions on or after 1 April 2004, a minimum rate of corporation tax of 19% will apply where a company whose profits are below the threshold for the small companies rate, distributes profits to a non-company shareholder.

The rates for the year to 31 March 2004 were the same. The profits charged to corporation tax include both income and capital gains.

Capital gains tax. Payable by individuals (subject to many exemptions and reliefs) at marginal rates of tax on capital profits in excess of £8,500 in 2005/06 (£8,200 in 2004/05) made on the sale or disposal of assets.

Inheritance tax. Payable on certain lifetime transfers and by the personal representatives of deceased persons on wealth passing on death. The tax begins when total capital passing on death or lifetime transfers exceeds £275,000 in 2005/06 (£263,000 for 2004/05). The rate of tax on lifetime transfers is 20% rising to 40% for transfers on death. There are many exemptions.

Rates and the Council Tax. A uniform business rate is payable by businesses on the assessed letting value of land and buildings, and the council tax is payable on domestic accommodation.

National Insurance contributions. Effectively a tax although not normally so regarded by the Government.

(b) Indirect taxes

Customs and Excise duties. Chargeable on certain dutiable goods imported and those produced in the UK, such as liquors and tobacco. Also various licence fees and stamp duties.

Value added tax (VAT). Administered by the Customs and Excise and chargeable on the sales value of goods and services, with many exemptions and zero-rated items. Payable through the whole chain of importers, producers and distributors, less tax on purchases, but ultimately borne by the consumer. Chargeable at 17½% by a business with a turnover of £60,000 from 1 April 2005 (previously £58,000 from 31 March 2004).

1.10 THE SCHEDULAR SYSTEM OF DIRECT TAXATION

The schedular system of direct taxation was originally introduced in 1803. The Income Tax (Trading and Other Income) Act 2005 (ITTOIA 2005) which entered into force on 6 April 2005 has abolished this system in so far as it applies to Income Tax - it does remain for the time being for Corporation Tax.

Schedules A, D, E and F are now referred to as property income, trading income, employment income and investment income in the hope that such terms are likely to be more meaningful to the layman.

Foreign sources of income are now included with their equivalent UK source rather than being classified separately, but with the special rules relating to foreign income being contained in a separate part of the Act.

2

Personal Taxation

2.1 ASSESSING THE LIABILITY

An individual is liable for income tax on the whole of his or her income which is chargeable to tax. That income may include, for example, remuneration from employment, business profit, rents from letting property or rooms, and income from investments. Very little income escapes the tax net. There may also be a liability for capital gains tax which is considered in Chapter 5.

From the gross income of a taxpayer from all sources, certain charges on income are deductible, such as eligible interest and royalties. Gifts and living expenses are not allowable deductions. Personal reliefs and allowances are then deducted from the remaining amount, called 'total income', to produce a balance on which income tax is charged, the 'taxable' income.

In 2003/04, income tax will be charged as described previously on page 21, but shown again here.

	2004/05		2005/06	
	Band £	Rate %	Band £	Rate %
Starting	0-2,020	10%	0-2,090	10%
Basic	2,021-31,400	22%	2,091-32,400	22%
Higher	over 31,400	40%	over 32,400	40%

For the purpose of calculating the higher rate payable, interest received net of tax and dividends must be 'grossed up'. Grossing up means calculating the amount of the interest or dividend by adding back tax which has been deducted.

The tax payable by an employed taxpayer or pensioner will normally be accounted for by PAYE deductions from the pay or occupational pension. However, the actual tax liability will often need re-calculation after the end of the tax year leaving an amount underpaid or overpaid. The adjustments may be due, for instance, to incorrect codings for PAYE, and the correction of estimates, e.g. state pensions, income from property and investment income, not taxed at source.

Business profits made by the self-employed or partners are included, with all other sources and income, on the self-assessment tax return (see 2.2 below).

2.2 SELF-ASSESSMENT

Readers who require specific guidance on how to complete their Self-Assessment Tax Return, should refer to the comprehensive Guide which accompanies the tax return. This will take you through the maze and lead to a successful and accurate completion of the return for which you are legally responsible.

It is possible to complete your self-assessment tax return on-line. There are also several organisations who offer on-line services for assessment, advice about tax coding and general tax saving. If you wish to follow this route, then an initial approach with a search engine such as Ask Jeeves will bring up quite a list of relevant sites (and some oddities). For information about self-assessment on-line, go direct to **www.inlandrevenue.gov.uk**. Some of the advantages of doing your self-assessment on-line are:

- automatic calculation of your tax as you complete the return
- internet returns are processed faster
- any money owed you by the IR is paid faster
- on-line acknowledgement of your return is given on receipt
- it is safe, secure and more convenient – the service can be used day or night
- the web pages provide comprehensive information and assistance in all aspects of self-assessment.

2.3 MINIMISING THE LIABILITY

Careful study of this chapter will indicate how in many cases an individual's tax liability can be reduced. This subject was discussed in Chapter 1, section 1.6, but is worth repetition. In particular consideration should be given to the following courses of action:

☑ Obtain all the possible reliefs and allowances.

☑ Take advantage of opportunities for tax-free investments, as discussed in Chapter 3, Investment Income.

☑ A married couple should ensure that no allowances are lost because one partner has insufficient taxable income. This could be achieved by, for example, transferring investments to the party with insufficient income, or ensuring that an adequate but defendable salary is paid to that party for services to a business carried out by the other partner. The transfer of investments may also be effective in reducing inheritance tax.

☑ One party's liability for higher rate tax may be reduced or eliminated by a transfer of income to the other party in the manner suggested above.

☑ For married couples still entitled to the married couple's allowance, the transfer of the married couple's allowance to the other tax-paying spouse may prevent it being lost. (See page 29 for details on persons eligible to claim married couple's allowance.)

☑ Where income is received from self-employment, part-time work or an unincorporated business owned by the taxpayer, ensure that all allowable expenses are charged in the business accounts.

☑ Where one party's potential capital gains are likely to exceed the annual threshold of £8,500 in 2005/06 (£8,200 in 2004/05), this would be another situation where a transfer of investments to the party with lower potential gains would be desirable. Since capital gains tax is payable at marginal income tax rates, such transfers would be particularly effective where the transferor is liable to tax at the higher rate, but the other party is not so liable.

2.4 SPECIMEN COMPUTATIONS

(a) Basic rate taxpayer

J Smith is a single man aged 30 with the following sources of income in 2005/06

	£
Income from employment	27,000
(PAYE deducted at source £4,610)	
Income from rented properties	3,650
Dividends (net)	900
Bank interest (net)	1,600

Mr Smith's tax liability for 2005/06 can be arrived at as follows:

	Non-savings Income £	Savings Income £	Dividend Income £	Tax deducted at source £
Employment earnings	27,000			4,610
Property income	3,650			
Dividends (10/9)			1,000	100
Taxed interest – bank interest (100/80)		2,000		400
Statutory Total Income	30,650	2,000	1,000	5,110
Single person's allowance	(4,895)			
Taxable income	25,755	2,000	1,000	

Tax:
	£
2,090 @ 10%	209.00
23,665 @ 22%	5,206.30
2,000 @ 20%	400.00
1,000 @ 10%	100.00
Tax borne	5,915.30
Less:	
Tax deducted at source and tax credit on dividend	(5,110.00)
Tax due	805.30

> **Editor's note**
>
> If you have last year's Taxation Simplified and you compare this computation with the similar one there, you will notice that Smith's tax liability is £1.40 less although he has earned £2,000 more. Interesting!

(b) Higher Rate Taxpayer

If Mr Smith's income from employment for the year had been £35,000 with PAYE deducted of £6,370, his tax liability would be arrived at as follows:

	Non-savings Income £	Savings Income £	Dividend Income £	Tax deducted at source £
Employment earnings	35,000			6,370
Property income	3,650			
Dividends (10/9)			1,000	100
Taxed interest – bank interest (100/80)		2,000		400
Statutory Total Income	38,650	2,000	1,000	6,870
Single person's allowance	(4,895)			
Taxable income	33,755	2,000	1,000	

Tax: £

	£
2,090 @ 10%	209.00
30,310 @ 22%	6,668.20
3,355 @ 40%	1,342.00
1,000 @ 32.5%	325.00
Tax borne	8,544.20
Less:	
Tax deducted at source and tax credit on dividend	(6,870.00)
Tax due	1,674.20

> **Editor's note**
>
> Likewise, you will notice that Smith's tax liability under these circumstances is £208.40 less although he has earned the same. Even more interesting! There are, of course, many other factors to consider, but overall, this year's demands for some people seem likely to be less than last year's.

2.5 RELIEFS AND ALLOWANCES

(a) Personal allowance

This allowance is available to persons of either sex (including children), whether married or not. Thus, under independent taxation, both husband and wife obtain the allowance. The allowance depends on the age of the taxpayer and is as follows:

	2002/03	2003/04	2004/05	2005/06
	£	£	£	£
Age below 65 years	4,615	4,615	4,745	4,895
65-74	6,100	6,610	6,830	7,090
75 and over	6,370	6,720	6,950	7,220

(b) Married couple's allowance, widow's bereavement allowance, and child allowance

From 6 April 2000, these allowances were mostly abolished. Only a small part of one allowance remains. The married couple's allowance is only available to taxpayers born before 6 April 1935. A married pensioner who was 65 on 5th April 2000 can claim it, but one who became 65 on 6th April 2000 cannot. A single pensioner who was 65 before 6th April 2000 who later marries can claim the married couple's allowance.

Married couple's allowance. (From 6 April 2000, pensioner couples only)
This allowance is given primarily to the husband but can be transferred to the wife, provided they are living together or he is responsible for her maintenance. A couple can choose to allocate the whole allowance to the wife, or she could claim, as of right, half the allowance. The tax relief on the allowance was restricted in 1999/00 to 10%. For subsequent years, please see opening paragraph above. A transfer would be an advantage where the husband could not use the allowance. The allowance is as follows:

	2002/03	2003/04	2004/05	2005/06
	£	£	£	£
Husband or wife 65-74	5,465	5,565	5,725	5,905
Husband or wife 75 plus	5,535	5,635	5,795	5,995

These allowances are reduced by half of the amount by which the taxpayer's income exceeds £19,500 in 2005/06 and £18,900 in 2004/05. The minimum allowance for 2005/06 is £2,280 and £2,210 in 2004/05.

Widow's bereavement allowance and child allowance have been abolished.

(c) Blind persons
If the taxpayer is registered as a blind person for the whole or part of a year, an allowance of £1,610 in 2005/06 and £1,560 in 2004/05 may be claimed. Where the allowance is not needed, it can in certain circumstances be transferred to the taxpayer's husband or wife. By concession, the allowance is available for the year previous to the year of registration on proof of blindness at the end of that previous year.

2.6 CHILDREN

Child benefits. These are cash payments payable to mothers in respect of children under 19 years of age (Child Benefit Act 1975). The payments are exempt from tax.

Where child benefits do not apply. Child benefits may not be payable in respect of children under 19 years of age living in certain overseas countries – for example, the former USSR, Asia, India, Pakistan, Africa and the Americas – where there are no reciprocal arrangements for social security benefits.

Scholarships. Income from a scholarship for full-time education is exempt from income tax so far as the holder of the scholarship is concerned. However, in the case of a scholarship paid for by the employer of a director or employee earning £8 500 p.a. or more, the cash value of a scholarship for a member of their family will normally be treated as part of their remuneration, subject to qualifications where payment is made from a trust fund.

Adopted children. By an extra-statutory concession in 1983, no tax will be charged on allowances paid to people who adopt children under government-approved schemes.

Child care. No tax is payable by an employee for the value of a place in a nursery provided by the employer for the employee's child. Tax is however payable by an employee on a cash allowance, voucher for child care or fees paid for child care if paid by the employer to the employee. Fees paid by the employer direct to nurseries, etc., and minders are taxable on directors and on employees earning £8,500 or more.

Two new tax credits

The Child Tax Credit and the Working Tax Credit were introduced from April 2003 to support families with children, tackle poverty and make work pay.

The **Child Tax Credit** brings together the various strands of support for families with children – the child elements in Income Support, Jobseeker's Allowance, Working Families' Tax Credit (WFTC), Disabled Person's Tax Credit (DPTC) and the Children's Tax Credit – into one streamlined system.

The **Working Tax Credit** broadly replicates the adult support in WFTC and extends the principles of WFTC and DPTC to adults without children to create one transparent instrument to make work pay, paid through the wage packet. It also includes support with the costs of childcare, building on the success of the existing childcare component of WFTC and DPTC.

The Child Tax Credit

Child Tax Credit is a payment to support families with children. Claims can be made by an individual, a couple or a polygamous family unit. There are no requirements to be working in order to make a claim.

A claim for Child Tax Credit must be made on form TC600. The same form is also used for claims for Working Tax Credit. Claim forms can be obtained from local Inland Revenue offices, or a form can be completed over the internet (**www.inlandrevenue.gov.uk/taxcredits**).

Child Tax Credit is paid for a child until 1 September following his or her 16th birthday, or for a young person aged 16 to 18 who is in full-time education, up to and including A-levels, NVQ level 3 or Scottish Highers, or a young person aged 16 to 18 who has left full-time education but does not have a job or training place and who has registered with the Careers Service.

Child Tax Credit is paid in addition to Child Benefit and any Working Tax Credit.

The amount of Child Tax Credit to which an individual, couple or family unit is entitled will be calculated by reference to the family income for the year of the claim. Claims for 2005/06 will be based initially on income figures for the year ended 5 April 2006. Persons claiming Child Tax Credit (or, for that matter, Working Tax Credit) will be required to complete a return at the end of each claim year, giving details of their actual income for that year. This information will be used to revise claims where necessary.

Child Tax Credit (CTC)		
	2004/05	2005/06
	£	£
Annual		
Family element (double in year of birth)*	545	545
Child element (per child)†		
- disabled child	3,840	3,975
- severely disabled child	4,730	4,895
- any other child	1,625	1,690

* Claim reduced by £1 for every £15 of annual income over £50,000
† Where only CTC available, claim reduced by 37p for every £1 of annual income over £13,910 (£13,480 in 2004/05); £5,000 where CTC also available

The Working Tax Credit

Working Tax Credit is designed to top up the earnings of working people on low incomes, whether or not they have children. It is available to employed or self-employed people and includes support for the costs of qualifying child care.

People who are responsible for a child or a young person can claim Working Tax Credit if they are over 16 and working at least 16 hours per week.

People without children can claim WTC provided:

- they are aged 25 or over and working at least 30 hours per week
- they are aged 16 or over and working at least 16 hours per week AND they have a disability which makes getting a job more difficult for them
- they are aged 50 or over and working at least 16 hours per week and are returning to work after time spent on qualifying out-of-work benefits.

Working Tax Credit is paid in addition to Child Tax Credit. The amount depends on the circumstances of the individual or couple.

Working Tax Credit (WTC)	2004/05 £	2005/06 £
Annual		
Basic element	1,570	1,620
Second adult or lone parent addition	1,545	1,595
30 hour element	640	660
Disability element	2,100	2,165
Severe disability element	890	920
Age 50+ element working 16-29 hours per week*	1.075	1,110
Age 50+ element working 30+ hours per week*	1,610	1,660
Weekly		
Childcare element		
- maximum eligible cost for 1 child	135	175
- maximum eligible cost for 2 or more children[†]	200	300

Claimants can be eligible for each element
Claim reduced by 37p for every £1 of annual income over £5,220

Mutually exclusive
[†]*Reduced to 70% of eligible cost*

Some general points to bear in mind with regard to the claiming of Tax Credits

- Claims for Tax Credits can only be backdated for a maximum of three months. This means that those people wishing to ensure that their claims run from 6 April 2005 must lodge their claims by 6 July 2005. This can create difficulties for people unsure as to whether they will qualify for Tax Credits in 2005/06. The Inland Revenue have indicated that they will accept protective claims for Tax Credits from persons uncertain as to what their circumstances for 2005/06 will entitle them.

- Tax Credits are worked out ultimately on the basis of annual average income NOT on an actual basis.

  Example: Mr B is single and is employed from 6 April 2004 to 6 October 2004 at a salary of £30,000 pa. He is made redundant with effect from 6 October 2004 and returns to work on 6 January 2005 on a salary of £24,000.

  For the purposes of calculating any entitlement to Tax Credits, Mr B's annual average income would be:

$$\begin{array}{ll} £30,000 \times 6/12 = & £15,000 \\ £24,000 \times 3/12 = & \underline{£6,000} \\ & £21,000 \end{array}$$

- The rules on Tax Credits require notifying the Inland Revenue of changes in circumstances within 3 months of the date of change. There are penalties (maximum £300) for failing to notify. Changes in circumstances that require notification to the Inland Revenue include:
  1. changes in the composition of the credit-claiming unit such as ceasing to be, or becoming, a member of a couple
  2. changes in the amount spent on childcare which give rise to a fall in average childcare costs of £10 a week or more, and which last for at least four weeks in a row.

- Changes in income do NOT have to be notified to the Inland Revenue within three months of the date of change, but people may wish to notify such changes to the Inland Revenue with a view to getting their claims revised as soon as possible.

- People who make a claim for Tax Credits should be aware that there is no provision for a Tax Credit claim once made, to be withdrawn. This means that, even if they do not qualify for Tax Credits, they must still keep the Inland Revenue informed of changes of circumstances, e.g. the birth of a child or commencement of childcare costs. They will also need to complete the end-of-year return providing details of the Tax Credit-claiming unit's joint income for the year. Thus there could be instances of significant compliance costs without any benefit in terms of being eligible to receive Tax Credits.

Child Trust Fund

A new Child Trust Fund is introduced through which the Government will provide an initial endowment of £250 (£500 for low income families) for all children born from September 2002. The fund has other features including:

- allowing additional contributions to be made by others such as parents, family and friends, of up to £1,200 per year
- accessible at age 18
- delivered through open market competition.

2.7 HUSBAND AND WIFE

In most circumstances the following particular rules apply:

- Each party obtains a personal allowance – £4,895 in 2005/06 (£4,745 in 2004/05), increased for those aged 65 and over.

- Income from property owned jointly by husband and wife is normally assumed to be shared equally. However, from 6 April 2004, income distributions from shares in a close company that are jointly owned by a married couple will no longer automatically be split 50:50, subject to an election for the split to be based on the actual proportion of ownership and entitlement to this income. Instead, distributions (usually dividends) will be taxed according to the actual proportions of ownership and entitlement to the income.

- If one party to a marriage was 65 on 5 April 2000, a married couple's allowance is claimable. The parties must be living together (or the husband be maintaining a separated wife) for this further allowance to apply. In the year of marriage, it is reduced by 1/12th for each month (beginning on the sixth of each month) before marriage.

- The whole or part of the allowance can be transferred to the wife.

- No transfer of excess allowances is available where the couple are separated, but where the husband is continuing to support the wife he will obtain the further allowance as above. This also applies in reverse.

Civil Partnerships

The Government has announced that Civil Partnerships formed as a result of the Civil Partnerships Act 2004 will be treated the same as married couples for tax purposes.

2.8 SALARIES, WAGES AND DIRECTORS' FEES

Introduction

For most people the greater part, if not the whole, of their income consists of the salary, wages, commission, bonuses and fees they draw under a contract of employment. This part of a taxpayer's income is assessed in accordance with the rules of the charge to tax on employment income. The most important of these rules are considered in this section.

The majority of tax on earnings from employment is collected by deduction under the Pay As You Earn (PAYE) system, which is considered later. Earnings are assessed as income for the year in which they are received – see below page 37.

There are different rules according to (a) whether the taxpayer is resident, ordinarily resident and domiciled in the UK and (b) where the duties of employment are carried out.

The Pay As You Earn system (PAYE)

(a) General

The following notes are intended to indicate only the general nature and scope of the PAYE system. More detailed information is available from Tax Offices where a comprehensive pamphlet, the Employer's Guide to PAYE, can be obtained.

PAYE is the system under which employers are obliged to deduct income tax and National Insurance contributions from their employees' remuneration. The amount to be deducted is found from tax tables which take into account, by a coding system, the reliefs and allowances to which each employee is entitled. The employee's code is notified by the tax office to the employer and to the employee who, in addition, receives details showing how this particular code is made up. The employee should ensure that he or she is receiving all the applicable reliefs and allowances.

The remuneration from which the deductions are made includes all income from the employment, including salaries, wages, holiday pay, bonuses, fees, commission, pensions (to retired employees), most sickness benefits and some taxable benefits provided by the employer, the amount of which must be notified to the employee.

In order to assist self assessment employers have to issue their employees a P60 by 31 May of each year.

(b) Benefits

In the case of most benefits provided by the employer, such as the provision of a company car, the benefit will be outside the PAYE deduction scheme. In those cases the benefit will be taken into account in the code, so that the tax collected under

PAYE will be increased by the necessary amount. Employers have to provide a copy of Form P11D to the employee by 6 July of each year.

(c) Deductions from pay

Where the remuneration is subject to deduction of the tax under PAYE, the amount to be taken into account is the amount before deductions, such as National Insurance Contributions (NIC) and allowable trade union subscriptions. However, where contributions to the employer's approved pension scheme are allowable, the amount of the contribution will reduce the amount of the pay on which PAYE is operated. Further payments subject to PAYE are redundancy pay where this is taxable, and certain advance payments of directors' fees.

An employee can arrange for contributions to approved charities to be deducted from remuneration and paid by the employer to specific charities, these contributions reducing pay for tax purposes.

(d) Refunds

When an employee has experienced a period of low remuneration, such as during sickness or unemployment, refunds may be due, but no refund can be made while an employee is involved in a trade dispute.

(e) Records

In addition to making correct deductions from employees' pay, an employer has to keep accurate records which may be inspected by tax officials, and submit annual returns; these returns include P11D forms showing the expenses and benefits of directors and employees receiving more than £8 500 p.a., and P9D forms showing expenses of other employees. An employer also has to provide employees with certificates of pay and tax deducted at the end of each tax year, and P45 forms with similar information when an employee leaves the employment.

(f) The codes

Apart from the issue of codes a tax office will not provide an employer with any information about an employee's affairs. The codes do, however, provide some information. Thus a code with the suffix H indicates that the taxpayer receives the married couple's allowance or the additional personal allowance; L indicates the personal allowance; codes P and V include the age allowance for single and married couples respectively. Where an employee does not wish this information disclosed he should apply for code T, which is used for special cases, such as where there is no 'free pay' (i.e. no allowances are given by the code OT) or, where no tax is deductible, code NT. The code BR indicates that the tax is deducted at the basic rate. The prefix D shows that higher rates are payable.

Code K

This applies where coding reductions exceed allowances. The coding reductions might cover occupational pensions, taxable benefits and untaxed income (e.g. on certain savings). Under the old code F the income in excess of the allowances was estimated and could only have the effect of reducing the allowances to nil. As a result the excess of the income over the allowances was subject to assessment at the end of the year. Under the K code such assessments should no longer be necessary as this new code deducts actual income (not estimated income) from the allowances, and if a surplus of income results that amount is added to pay or occupational pension.

Receipts basis of taxing remuneration

(a) General. From 6 April 1989 employees, including directors, have been taxed for a tax year on the remuneration actually received, or assumed to be received in that year. The new basis did not change the system for taxing regular payments of salaries and wages which were already taxed on a receipts basis and were subject to deductions for PAYE. It did, however, affect remuneration which is paid in a tax year after the year in which it is earned. This is often the case where directors' fees and bonuses are dependent on profits and cannot therefore be determined or paid until after the end of the accounting year of the business.

(b) Time of receipt of remuneration. It will be assumed that an individual has received remuneration at the earliest of the following times:

- When payment is made.
- When the employee or director becomes entitled to payment (which may be after the accounting year in which the remuneration is earned). In the case of directors:
  (i) when remuneration is credited to an employee's or director's account with the paying company – this often happens in smaller companies, where it is the practice to credit remuneration or fees of directors to their current account, and to pay part or all of the balance on that account when the cash position permits
  (ii) where remuneration is determined during the course of an accounting year, it is assumed to be received at the end of that year
  (iii) where remuneration for an accounting period is determined after the end of that period, it will be taxed in the fiscal year when it is determined.
- Chargeable benefits are to be treated as received for tax purposes when the benefits are provided.

These rules apply to PAYE deductions.

(c) Treatment in business computation. Remuneration charged in the business accounts in a particular accounting year is, of course, normally an allowable deduction in computing profits for that year. However, if remuneration is paid nine months or more after the end of an accounting period in which it is charged, that remuneration is not deductible in computing that year's taxable profit. It will be observed that where this rule applies the taxable profit for the year when the remuneration arises will be so much greater than the accounts profit.

If a tax calculation is made within the nine-month period, and the remuneration has not then been paid, that remuneration will be disallowed in the calculation, and allowed later when the remuneration is paid. However, the calculation can be adjusted if the remuneration is subsequently paid within the nine-month period; but a claim for this purpose must be made to the Inspector of Taxes within two years of the end of the accounts period concerned.

Compensation for loss of employment

If the compensation arises out of the contract of employment it is taxable in the hands of the recipient, unless paid for disability or injury, special contributions to approved retirement schemes, foreign service (with conditions) and terminal grants to members of the armed forces. By a statutory concession dated 2 September 1993 legal costs received as a result of pursuing a claim are not taxable. Voluntary payments made to an employee after his employment has ceased are exempt from tax up to £30,000. Statutory redundancy pay is also exempt, but does use up part or all of the £30,000 exempt amount.

2.9 TAXABLE BENEFITS

General

Liability to tax may arise on benefits provided for an employee in addition to his salary, and these benefits may be in kind rather than cash. Particular examples of taxable benefits include the use of company cars, free accommodation, loans at beneficial rates, the provision of suits and television sets and free travel and credit card payments.

The general principle is that the cash equivalent of the benefits will be assessed on directors, and on employees earning £8,500 or more (including the value of the benefits). The rules do not apply to full-time working directors earning less than £8,500 who, with their relatives and associates (e.g. partners), own no more than 5% of the company's share capital. Employees earning less than £8,500 may be assessed on benefits received if such benefits are convertible into cash. The cash equivalent will in most cases be the cost to the employer, less any reimbursement by the employee.

The case of Pepper v. Hart, 1993, established that the cost of a benefit shall for tax purposes be based on the marginal, not average, cost. Marginal cost means essentially the additional cost to the employer for providing the benefit. It is likely that there will be problems in arriving at marginal cost and that some of these problems will be resolved by legislation or statements of Inland Revenue practice. Pepper v. Hart specifically concerned the benefit obtained by teachers who obtained places at reduced fees for their children in schools where the teachers were employed; in these cases the Inland Revenue has announced that no benefit will arise for payments of at least 15% of normal fees. Likewise it is accepted that the marginal cost of employees' travel in transport undertakings is nil where passengers paying normal fares are not displaced; and company goods sold to employees at not less than the wholesale price will not produce taxable benefits.

In the case of an asset placed at the disposal of a director, or employee earning more than £8,500, or members of their families, the cost is deemed to be the annual value of the benefit. The annual value of accommodation is the letting value.

From 5 April 1990 no tax has been charged on the benefit for higher paid employees on nursery facilities provided by employers.

Returns of benefits in kind for directors and higher-paid employees are made on form P11D, but for certain expenses a dispensation can be obtained from reporting on this form.

Business cars

(a) General. Taxpayers receive a benefit from the private use of business cars and this benefit is, in general, taxable; conversely, taxpayers can obtain tax allowances for the business use of their private cars. The treatment for tax purposes differs according to whether the taxpayer using the car is self-employed, an employee earning under £8,500 a year, a director or an employee earning £8,500 p.a. and above. The Inland Revenue is authorised to supply lists to the DSS of employers liable for Class 1A National Insurance contributions on these benefits.

(b) Employees (not directors) earning under £8,500 p.a. No taxable benefit is chargeable for the use of a car provided by the employer, provided some use of the car is made for business. However, the figure of £8,500 includes all the potentially taxable benefits.

(c) Self-employed persons. Capital allowances up to £3,000 p.a. may be obtained for vehicles used for business purposes, but these allowances will be reduced by the proportionate private mileage of the vehicle. Likewise the cost of fuel, maintenance, insurance and tax charged in the business accounts will need to be reduced for private use of the vehicle.

(d) Volunteer drivers. Volunteer drivers are liable for tax on any profit made on mileage allowances received from hospitals and similar volunteer organisations.

The profit is the excess of the mileage allowances received over the Inland Revenue estimate of the cost per mile of running and maintaining the car.

(e) Car Benefits

- From 6 April 2002, taxable benefits for cars are based on a percentage of their list price, graduated according to their levels of CO_2 emissions.
- Minimum benefits will be 15% of list price where CO_2 emission does not exceed 140 g/km for 2005/06.
- The minimum will increase by 1% for each g/km of extra CO_2 emissions, subject to a maximum of 35% of list price.
- Diesel cars will be subject to 3% supplement (maximum of 35%).
- Cars with no CO_2 emission or registered before 1 January 1998 will be assessed on engine size.
- Discounts are available for environmentally friendly cars.

Disabled drivers

The cost of converting a company car for use by a disabled person is no longer included in the price of the car for car benefit purposes.

Car fuel scale charges

From 2003/04 onwards, a new system was introduced to calculate car fuel benefit for employees receiving free fuel for private mileage in company cars.

The way in which the benefit is measured is directly linked to the CO_2 emissions of the company car. The same percentage used to calculate car benefit is applied to calculate fuel benefit. This percentage is then multiplied against a set figure for the year. This set figure is £14,400 for both 2005/06 and 2004/05.

The set percentages are increased by 3 points for diesel cars (subject to a maximum of 35%) and there are discounts for alternative fuelled cars.

As was the case under the previous rules, no charge applies if the employee is required to make good to the employer the cost of all fuel used for private purposes and does, in fact, do so.

A standard charge of £500 is taxable where a van is provided by an employer for the private use of an employee. For vans four years old at the end of the tax year the benefit is reduced to £350. The benefit is reduced proportionately for vans incapable of being used for 30 days in a year. A van can be a car converted to carry goods or tools, etc. This would be by the removal of the rear seats, seat belts, etc. It has to be incapable of being reconverted in less than an 'evening'.

From 6 April 2005, a nil charge will apply to employees who have to take their vans home and are not allowed to use them for any other private use. Where private use is unrestricted, the £500 or £350 rules will continue to apply.

From 6 April 2007, a van with unrestricted private use will have a flat benefit of £3,000, irrespective of the age of the van. Moreover, if an employer provides fuel for unrestricted private use, an additional fuel charge of £500 will also apply.

Company cars sold to employees. The employee may be liable for tax on the excess of the market value over the price at which the car is sold to him. This particularly applies to cars previously leased to customers.

Employees' transport – general rules. If an employee is necessarily obliged to use his own car on his employer's business, the employee can deduct the expenses of doing so from any reimbursement he receives from the employer. The reimbursement normally takes the form of a mileage rate. Any surplus which results is taxable in the employee's hands and a deficiency is a tax-allowable deduction from the employee's earnings. It is interesting to note that these rules also apply to the use of the employee's horse and bicycle at 12p per mile and motorcycle at 24p! It is, however, necessary to record and justify records of business and private mileage and of the expenses incurred, the expenses being apportioned on the basis of the proportionate business mileage. Obviously difficulties arise in keeping accurate records and for this reason the Authorised Mileage Rates Scheme, explained below, is easier to operate.

Cash alternative – When the use of a company car was readily convertible into cash by the employee (i.e. a director and those earning £8,500 a year or more) the cash equivalent was chargeable to tax in the employee's hands. The employer is liable to pay Class 1A National Insurance contributions on the benefit (TA 1988 S.19). If the employee receives a higher salary instead of the use of a company car that employee will, in the normal course, be liable to tax on the higher salary. Even in the case where an option to take a higher salary is offered by the employer, the employee will pay tax on the option of the higher salary (Heaton v Bell 1969).

Authorised Mileage Rates – From 6 April 2002, a new system of flat rate mileage allowances was introduced for employees using their own transport for business journeys. Employers no longer need to report mileage payments up to their authorised rates, and dispensations will no longer apply.

The rates are as follows:

Cars and vans
First 10,000 miles in any tax year	40p per mile
Additional miles over 10,000	25p per mile
Motorcycles	24p per mile
Bicycles	20p per mile

Prior to April 2002, employees could claim tax-free mileage allowances for business use of their own cars, according to the scale shown below.

The 'tax-free' rates which applied for business mileage were as follows. Those for 1997/98 to 2000/01 are shown in brackets:

Size of car engine	on the first 4,000 miles in the tax year	on each mile over 4,000 miles in the tax year
up to 1 000 cc	40p (28p)	25p (17p)
1 000 – 1 500 cc	40p (35p)	25p (20p)
1 500 – 2 000 cc	45p (45p)	25p (25p)
over 2 000 cc	63p (63p)	36p (36p)

If the employee receives from the employer a mileage rate greater than the sum above, the employee will be taxed on the excess. Any deficit between the amount received and the above rates or (prior to 6 April 2002 only) actual costs incurred can be claimed against tax. Relief for interest on loans to buy the transport is not allowed with effect from 6 April 2002.

Gifts, gratuities and parties

In general, gifts are taxable in the hands of employees if they arise out of the employment. Typical examples of taxable gifts are tips, footballers' benefits and Christmas gifts. Gift vouchers are assessable at their cost to the employer, but luncheon vouchers for no more than 15p a day are not assessable; nor are meals in a canteen available for employees generally or long-service awards to employees up to £50 per year of service (in 2002/03 £20 per year). Gifts to employees by third parties are not taxable up to £250 (to 5 April 2003 £150) p.a., nor is entertainment provided by third parties. Modest expenditure on staff parties, e.g. at Christmas, is not regarded as a benefit if less than £150 per person (£75 in 2002/03). The expenditure, from 6 April 1995, may be spent on more than one event as long as the total is not exceeded. If one function costs more than £150 per head the whole amount is assessed. If more than £150 is spent on more than one event or function, it is those functions which take the expenditure over £150 and beyond which are assessable.

Gift aid

Charitable gifts by individuals and close companies qualify for tax relief. From 6 April 2000, there is no longer a minimum.

From 6 April 2000, the upper limit on gifts deducted from wages is abolished.

For gifts made under Gift Aid after 5 April 2003, donors may elect to have the donation treated as though made in the previous year of assessment.

From April 2004, taxpayers can nominate a charity to receive all or part of any tax repayment due to them. The nomination is made on the taxpayer's self-assessment form.

Accommodation

Where an employee is provided with a house or other accommodation rent free or at a rent below the gross rateable annual value, he or she will normally be liable to pay tax on the annual value, reduced by the rent the employee pays. This does not apply to employees such as caretakers who are required to live in the accommodation as part of their duties, but the only directors who can obtain the advantage of this exemption are full-time working directors, or directors of non-profit-making companies, and they must have no material interest in the company. Accommodation provided for directors where there is a threat to their security is also exempt. The cost of heating, lighting, cleaning, repairs (other than structural repairs), maintenance, decoration, furniture and domestic effects, which is not met by the employee, must not exceed 10% of his or her emoluments.

Where an employee first occupies the house provided by his or her employers on and after 31 March 1983, and the cost of providing the accommodation exceeds £75,000, the employee may be liable for tax at the official rate of interest on the excess. Where the property has been held for six years before the employee's occupation, the cost becomes the market value with vacant possession.

From 1990/91 and onwards, companies cannot reclaim VAT on the provision of free accommodation for directors or their families.

Relocation: employees moving house

From 5 April 1993 an employer may make a tax-free contribution of up to £8,000 for removal expenses of employees; the relief applies even if the employee retains the existing house, such as for letting. Relief for additional housing costs is withdrawn. The payments are not subject to PAYE but those over £8,000 must be recorded by the employer on forms P9D or P11D.

Business expenses

In the case of directors, and employees earning more than £8,500, the expenses or expense allowances paid by the business are assessable on the individual. It is then necessary for the employee or director to satisfy the Inspector of Taxes that the expenses were incurred for the purpose of the business.

From 6 April 1995 tax relief applies to certain incidental personal expenses paid by employers in respect of employees who are obliged to stay away from their homes overnight for business purposes. The most common such expenses include newspapers, telephone charges and laundry. The allowable amounts are £5 a night in the UK and £10 a night overseas. Payments above these limits are wholly chargeable to tax.

Beneficial loans

Where a loan is made by a business to an employee earning above £8,500, or a director, the individual will be chargeable to tax on the annual amount of interest below an 'official rate' to be notified by statutory instrument.

From 1994/95 and onwards, tax exemption applies where an employee's cheap or interest-free loans total no more than £5,000.

By concession an employee is not chargeable with tax on the benefit of cheap interest on a 'bridging loan' from his or her employer obtained because he or she had to change his residence owing to being transferred in the organisation. This concession applies to a loan outstanding for up to 12 months and not exceeding £30,000.

Income tax is not payable by employees on loans from employers whose business includes the lending of money, provided the loan is made on the same terms as are available to the public, ignoring differences in initial fees of administration (FA 1994).

Home-working

The 2003 Budget included proposals to allow employers to contribute towards additional household costs incurred by an employee who works at home, some or all of the time, under agreed flexible working arrangements without it giving rise to a change to income tax.

Employers can pay up to £2 per week without the need for supporting evidence of the costs the employee incurred. Where the employer pays more than that amount, evidence is needed to show that the payment is wholly in respect of additional household expenses incurred by the employee in carrying out his duties at home.

Medical insurance

The cost of medical insurance provided by an employer is assessable on directors and employees earning above £8,500. From 1982/83, this benefit is not taxable for employees earning under £8,500 p.a., and is in no case taxable for work overseas.

Statutory Maternity Pay (SMP)

Under the Employee Protection Act 1975 maternity pay can be paid to an employee after the employee ceases to work due to pregnancy. These payments are taxable as income from employment if the contract of employment still exists, and tax is deducted. If the contract of employment has been terminated at the time of payment, tax is chargeable as other income, and the payments may be made gross.

Season tickets

From 1982/83, the value of season tickets for travel to work provided by employers for employees is assessable on the employees, but loans made by employers for employees to buy season tickets are generally exempt.

Credit cards

From 1982/83, the value of purchases under credit cards made payable and chargeable to employers is taxable in the hands of the employees.

Armed Forces leave travel

Warrants or allowances for leave travel by members of the armed forces are exempt from tax.

Employer-supported childcare

The 2003 pre-Budget Report announced that from 6 April 2005 employees will be able to receive up to £50 per week of childcare, free of tax and National Insurance, provided employers contract with an approved childcarer or provide vouchers to pay an approved carer. To qualify, the benefit must be available to all employees.

2.10 LIABILITY INSURANCE AND UNINSURED LIABILITIES

On and after 6 April 1995 liability insurance on work-related risks is tax-free for employees and gives tax relief when paid for by employers. The tax-free relief applies for 6 years after the end of the employment. Also tax-free are payments for uninsured work-related charges which could have been insured, and these charges could include legal costs in defending an action.

2.11 LIFE ASSURANCE

To 13 March 1984. Policies made up to this date, and not subsequently amended, provide relief from income tax by means of a deduction of 12.5% from 6 April 1989 (previously 15%) from the premium payments. For the purpose of this relief the premiums could not exceed the greater of one sixth of the taxpayer's net income after charges, or £1,500 in a tax year.

After 13 March 1984. The above relief is withdrawn for policies taken out after this date and for existing policies where the benefits are subsequently improved.

2.12 NATIONAL INSURANCE AND SOCIAL SECURITY

Details of the current National Insurance contributions and benefits are obtainable from various pamphlets issued by the Department of Social Security. Contributions are divided into four classes, as follows:

Class 1. Employed persons.
Class 2. Self-employed persons.
Class 3. Voluntary contributions.
Class 4. Earnings-related contributions payable by the self-employed on earnings above a minimum, in addition to Class 2 contributions.

The contributions do not give relief from income tax. Employers' contributions under Class 1 are, however, deductible charges in computing taxable profits. Class 1a contributions are made by employers who provide a range of benefits or refund expenses to directors and higher-paid employees. For a comprehensive guide, please see the excellent Inland Revenue guide on Class 1 (CWG5 – 2002).

The rates and thresholds are set out below.

	2004/05	*2005/06*
Primary threshold	£91 p wk	£94 p wk
Secondary threshold	£91 p wk	£94 p wk
Employees' primary class 1 rate on earnings between primary threshold and upper earnings limit	11%	11%
Employees' primary class 1 rate on earnings above upper earnings limit	1%	1%
Employers' secondary class 1 rate on earnings above secondary threshold	12.8%	12.8%
Lower profits limit (for self-employed Class 4 contribution)	£4,745	£4,895
Class 4 rate on profits between lower and upper profits limit	8%	8%
Class 4 rate on profits above upper profits limit	1%	1%

Social security benefits

(a) Taxable. Retirement pension, widow's pensions and allowances; statutory sick pay (see below); statutory maternity pay; guardians and special allowances for children. The Job Seekers Allowance, excepting the earnings-related supplement and benefits to strikers' families, is taxable. Incapacity benefit is taxable except for the first 28 weeks and except where paid to persons receiving the former invalidity benefit at 12 April 1995 for the same incapacity

(b) Not taxable. Child benefit, benefits for sickness benefit (but not statutory sick pay), maternity, invalidity, industrial injury; mobility allowance; death grant; income support; housing credit; attendance allowance; family credit; supplementary benefits and pensions for wounds or disability payable to members of the armed forces, merchant seamen, and to civilians for war injury; war widows' pensions; and child dependency allowances. The Job Finder's grant is tax-free.

(c) Statutory sick pay (SSP). This is a payment which an employer is bound to make to most employees for absence due to sickness from 4 days to up to 28 weeks in a tax year. It forms part of the employee's income for tax and National Insurance purposes.

Employers do not require medical evidence before paying SSP.

Married women paying reduced rates of NI contributions are entitled to SSP.

The following are not entitled to SSP:

- Where other state benefits have been received.
- Where the maximum entitlement of SSP has been received.
- Those on strike.

In addition to the statutory entitlement to SSP an employee may be entitled to what is called 'occupational sick pay' (OSP) from the employer under his or her contract of service or custom in the employment. The rules of OSP may involve a deduction for SSP and state sickness benefits. Payments of OSP are also taxable in the employee's hands, except to the extent that the employee has contributed to a fund for the purpose.

The detailed rules for the calculation and eligibility for SSP can be complicated in particular cases and further information can be obtained from the Department of Social Security.

(d) Unemployment and strikes – Job Seeker's Allowance (JSA). The Job Seeker's Allowance, received by the unemployed person and one adult dependant (e.g. wife, husband, parent), is taxable and forms part of the taxpayer's total income for tax purposes in a tax year. Additions for children are not taxable.

Where the unemployment is prolonged, and the total income including JSA is consequently small, a refund of tax already paid (e.g. under PAYE) may be due. This would apply if the total income in a tax year to 5 April was below the personal and other allowances to which the taxpayer was entitled. This refund could not be obtained while benefit was being paid but would be paid soon after the next 5 April or, possibly, if the taxpayer obtained employment before that date.

As no tax is deducted from the benefits, and if the taxpayer's other income is sufficiently high, he or she might be liable for unpaid tax at the end of the tax year. This unpaid amount would be collected in the following tax year, usually by adjustment to the PAYE code if the taxpayer was then in employment.

Supplementary benefit for persons who do not have to make themselves available for employment is not taxable. Such persons include those over retirement age, single parents of children under 16, and those looking after disabled people.

Persons on strike. No benefit is payable to persons on strike, but supplementary benefit may be payable to a wife and this benefit is taxable. Tax is not deducted from the benefit. If any refund of tax is due it cannot be paid until the taxpayer returns to work, and if there is additional tax payable it will be recovered by adjustment to the taxpayer's PAYE coding for a future year. In all cases the tax payable for a tax year will be assessed soon after 5 April at the year end.

2.13 CHARITABLE GIVING

With effect from 6 April 2000, deeds of covenant were brought within the Gift Aid scheme. No Gift Aid declaration is required in respect of deeds of covenant executed before 6 April 2000.

One-off payments of any amount can be made to charities under the Gift Aid scheme, provided a Gift Aid declaration is made. Such a declaration may cover any number of donations already made or about to be made.

Declarations can be made in writing, by telephone, over the internet or orally – the essential point being that the charity obtains the donor's name and address.

Tax relief on Gift Aid is given at the payer's highest rate of tax. Basic rate relief is given by the donor deducting tax at source. Higher rate relief is given by extending the basic rate band by the gross amount of the payment.

Example:

Mr A makes a payment of £78 to charity. He is a higher rate taxpayer. For 2005/06, Mr A's basic rate will be £32,400 + (£78 x 100/78) = £32,500. The gross payment of £100 is not deducted in calculating Statutory Total Income.

Income tax relief is also available in respect of gifts of shares to charity. Such shares must be listed on a recognised stock exchange. The donor may deduct 'the relevant amount' from his income in calculating Statutory Total Income. The relevant amount is the market value of the shares at the date of the gift.

2.14 INTEREST PAID AND HOME LOANS

Summary

In general, interest payable by an individual on a debt or a loan, including hire purchase and overdraft interest, is not an allowable charge against his or her income for tax purposes. However, interest paid does give tax relief in the following cases: loans for the purchase of homes up to 5 April 2000; loans for business purposes; purchase of retirement annuities where the loan is charged on property; and letting of residential accommodation. These cases are considered briefly below.

Home loans

From 6 April 2000, this relief is abolished.

Loans for business

Interest paid is an allowable expense where the loan is used for business purposes, including the interest on hire purchase transactions. Interest is also allowable in the following special cases:

- Loans for buying shares in partnership or loans to the partnership; this also applies to co-operatives. The borrower need not be an active member of the partnership.

- Loans for acquiring ordinary shares in close companies or for loans to close companies (not investment companies). A close company is one controlled by five or less 'participators', meaning generally shareholders. The participator, his or her relatives and associates (e.g. partners), count as one person for this purpose. To qualify the borrower must either (i) own more than 5% of the ordinary shares in the company, or (ii) own some shares and work full-time in the company.

- Loans for enabling employees to acquire ordinary shares in an employee-controlled company. The employee or his or her spouse must work full-time in the company. The company must be resident in the UK, must be a trading company and 'unquoted', i.e. there is no quotation for its shares on a Stock Exchange, and 75% of its ordinary shares, and the voting power, must be in the hands of the employees or their spouses. Other conditions apply.

The relief is withdrawn where the entity of the borrower changes, except where the loan could have been treated as a new loan to the new business entity.

Loans to buy retirement annuities

Tax relief is available on interest on the first £30,000 of a pre 9 March 1999 loan to a borrower aged 65 or more to purchase a life annuity, the loan being secured on the borrower's home.

Loans for let property

Relief on the interest is available provided that the property is let for at least 26 weeks in a year at a commercial rent.

Loans to directors and higher-paid employees

Where directors and employees earning over £8,500 a year receive loans from their employers at interest below a commercial rate the saving in interest is treated as a benefit and taxable as earnings from employment.

By concession an employee is not chargeable with tax on the benefit of cheap interest on a 'bridging loan' from the employer obtained because he or she had to change residence owing to being transferred in the organisation. This concession applies to a loan outstanding for up to 12 months and not exceeding £30,000.

2.15 PROVIDING FOR RETIREMENT

General

From 6 April 2001, the following changes were introduced.

(a) The self-employed pay contributions net of 22% basic rate tax (previously paid gross). An additional claim for higher rate tax relief must be made on the Self-Assessment tax return.
(b) The stakeholder pension scheme allows for contributions of £3,600 p.a. irrespective of income or contributions to other schemes or limits.

Provisions for retirement fall under the following: (a) National Insurance retirement pensions; (b) occupational pensions operated by employers; (c) additional voluntary contributions (AVC) which supplement an employer's scheme; and (d) personal pension plans (PPP). The legislation is complex, particularly so far as (b), (c) and (d) are concerned, but the essentials are set out below.

The Government has announced that the rules for tax-approved pension schemes will change radically from 6 April 2006. The new rules will be based on a single lifetime fund limit set at £1.5 million in 2006, increasing to £1.6 million in 2007, £1.65 million in 2008, £1.75 million in 2009 and £1.8 million in 2010. Transitional rules will provide some protection to those who are over the limit at the outset.

National Insurance retirement pensions

The various classes of contribution were referred to in section 2.12 above. Full information as to the current contributions and the pension entitlements in various individual circumstances can be obtained from pamphlets issued by the Department of Social Security. No tax relief is given on contributions. Employers' contributions are tax-allowable deductions in computing business profits. The retirement pension forms part of the pensioner's total income for tax purposes; i.e. it is taxable, assuming the recipient is liable for tax. Basic rate tax is not, however, deducted from the pension because many retired people are not liable for tax.

A National Insurance pension paid to a wife forms part of her taxable income even though it was derived from her husband's contributions.

Employer's occupational pension schemes

These are pension schemes set up by employers for the benefit of their employees and are administered by trustees including employee representatives. Contributions to the fund are usually made by both employer and employee but in some cases only by the employer. In order that the tax benefits shall be obtained the schemes must conform to certain conditions and be approved by the Occupational Pensions Board.

Subject to these conditions, the income of the fund is tax-free, the employer's contributions are allowable expenses in computing business profits, and the employee's contributions are deducted from remuneration before calculating his or her tax. The pension payable is taxable as earned income and tax is normally deducted from the payment according to the pensioner's code number.

For the tax benefits to be obtained, the pension must be no more than two thirds of final salary with a maximum cap of £105,600 in 2005/06 (£102,000 in 2004/05). These limits apply to new schemes established after 14 March 1989, and to employees entering existing schemes after 1 June 1989. However, pensions and lump sums in excess of these limits can be paid, for practical purposes involving separate funds, but the income of the separate funds and the contributions to them will not be eligible for tax relief. The schemes can provide for employees to retire at age 50 but 20 years' membership of the scheme is necessary for full relief. On leaving an employment, contributions are returnable to an employee with less than two years' membership of the scheme.

Pensions can provide for increases in the cost of living even though such increases take the pension above two thirds of the salary limit. Pensions to people who retire early because of ill health can be based on the length of service which could otherwise have been complete.

Additional voluntary contributions (AVC)

From October 1987 additional voluntary contributions to increase pensions (but not lump sums) may be paid by employees, either to the employer's pension scheme or to a 'free-standing' scheme of the employee's choice. Contributions may be made up to 15% of earnings (less payments to the employer's main scheme), subject to limits where earnings exceed £102,000 in 2004/05 (£99,000 in 2002/03). These additional contributions have the same tax benefits as for the main occupational pension scheme. The excess provided by the AVC will be refunded to the employee at retirement subject to tax at 10% above the employee's top rate, i.e. at 20% 32% or 50%, depending on total income.

Personal pension plans (PPP)

(a) **General nature of PPPs**. These are schemes which, from 1 July 1988, were established by individuals to provide pensions and lump sum benefits with important tax reliefs. The legislation, now contained in Chapter III of the Taxes Act 1988 (as amended by the Finance Act 1989), applies to all new personal pension schemes although, of course, existing retirement annuity contracts remain valid. Personal pensions can be arranged with authorised bodies, including insurance companies, banks, building societies, unit trusts, etc., and individuals may have freedom to manage the investment of their contributions. The schemes must have Inland Revenue approval and are subject to many conditions of which the essentials are outlined below.

(b) The contributors. Personal pension plans were initially introduced to provide tax incentives to the self-employed, and employees not covered by a company occupational pension scheme, to make pension provision for themselves. Employers who do not operate company schemes, such as many small businesses, can contribute to the PPPs of their employees.

(c) The benefits. The schemes may provide for both annuities and lump sums on retirement, and provision can be made for spouses and dependents. The benefits can be paid when the subscriber is aged 50 to 75, but may be paid earlier than 50 in the case of infirmity or where customary in the occupation. They may be arranged for up to a fixed term of 10 years even if the subscriber dies within that period. The lump sum must be paid when the pension becomes due, and is limited to 25% of the accumulated benefits with a maximum of £150,000 (1989/90 and onwards). The actual benefits will be calculated on what is called 'money purchase' of the fund, i.e. what the scheme will buy at maturity.

An annuity may be deferred until the annuitant reaches age 75, but amounts roughly comparable with the annuity may be withdrawn. Deferral of an annuity may be appropriate in times when annuity rates are low. The annuity can be provided by both UK insurers and by those in the European Union.

(d) The contribution limits. One of the main revisions of the rules for PPP contributions after 6 April 2001 is that individuals can make payments into a PPP of up to £3,600 per annum, regardless of earnings. This means that even children can start, or have started for them, a PPP. Payments are made net of basic rate tax and the pension company recovers basic rate tax from the Inland Revenue. Payments can also be made on behalf of another or out of capital.

Where individuals have net relevant earnings (NRE), it may be possible to pay higher pension contributions based on a set percentage of NRE according to the age of the individual. Net relevant earnings are effectively total earned income less the sum of excess trade charges over other income, loss relief and allowable deductions from employment income. The maximum PPP payable in any tax year will be the relevant percentage of the individual's NRE in that tax year or any of the five preceding tax years. For these purposes, NRE in years prior to 2001/02 can be taken into account.

For contributions in 2005/06, the taxpayer must advise the pension company receiving his or her payments of the NRE of the basis year, which would be the best year out of 2000/01 to 2005/06 inclusive.

For contributions paid after 5 April 2001, a one-year carry back of premiums is allowed provided an irrevocable election is made at or before the date of payment and before 31 January in the year following. For example, contributions paid before 31 January 2005 could be carried back and treated as if in the year to 5 April 2004, provided the appropriate election is made.

It is no longer possible to carry forward unused relief after 5 April 2001.

(e) Tax reliefs. Within the limits indicated above the contributions give relief of tax to the subscriber, basic rate income tax being deducted from the payments. The income from the invested fund is free of income tax and capital gains tax. A lump sum paid out of the value of the fund on maturity is free of income tax and inheritance tax. The value of the fund on maturity may be converted into an annuity from an insurance company, and the consequent yearly payments of the annuity form part of the earned income of the annuitant and are taxable. The lump sum is calculated after providing for dependents' benefits. Higher rate tax relief is obtained by increasing the taxpayer's basic rate band by the amount of the gross contribution.

(f) Assignment. Although a personal pension plan can include provision for dependents, the benefits cannot be assigned. The exception is where the accumulated fund is converted into an annuity for a fixed term and in this case the payments of the annuity after the death of the subscriber can be bequeathed by will.

Because of the tax reliefs, personal pension plans should represent good long-term investments. As means of providing for retirement they are particularly desirable for the self-employed and others not adequately covered by occupational pension schemes.

However, because contributions to occupational pension schemes are normally paid by employers, as well as employees, such schemes are often more beneficial.

3

Savings Income

General

For individuals with taxable income below the basic rate threshold of £32,400 (£31,400 for 2004/05), most investment income is charged to tax at 20% except for dividend income, which carries a tax credit of 10% of the gross dividend. Basic rate taxpayers have no further tax to pay in respect of such income.

Higher rate taxpayers are chargeable to tax at 40% on non-dividend savings income and 32.5% on dividend income. They therefore have further tax to pay of 20% on non-dividend savings income and 22.5% on dividend income. Where interest is received gross, there will be further tax to pay of 40%.

We now move on to consider specific types of savings income in more detail.

Taxed interest

Subject to the exceptions indicated below, interest received by the taxpayer is normally a net amount after the payer has deducted tax at the 20% rate. It includes interest received on company debentures, most government securities, local authority loans, other loans and deposits in building societies and banks. The taxpayer must enter the gross amount before tax on the return of income and it is the gross amount which forms part of the total income for the purpose, for example, of calculating any liability to higher-rate tax. If the taxpayer is not liable to tax or if the taxpayer's top rate of tax is the 10% band and they have suffered tax at 20% on interest received, they can recover the excess.

Untaxed interest

This refers to interest received without deduction of tax and would include interest from National Savings, government stock on the National Savings and Trustee Savings Bank registers, and 3½% War Loan. Tax is payable by assessment on untaxed interest, but it is particularly suitable for those not liable to tax, including charities. Individuals who are not liable for income tax can apply for interest to be paid gross. From 6 April 1996 tax on these sources is only liable at 20% if any tax is due.

Taxed dividends

In the case of dividends, i.e. shares of profit received from limited companies, the situation is similar to that of taxed interest; the lower rate is said to be 'imputed' to the dividend. Up to 5 April 1999 this meant that the person receiving the dividend was assumed to have suffered tax at 20%. Higher-rate taxpayers would be liable for tax at 40% on the grossed-up dividend, less the tax credit of 20%, i.e. a net payment of 20%. If an individual's total tax liability was less than the tax imputed to dividend income, and deducted from taxed interest, etc., the excess could be reclaimed.

From 1999/00, the tax credit on dividends was reduced to 10%, but cannot be reclaimed if the individual's total tax liability is less than the tax credit. The 10% tax credit will continue to satisfy the tax liability at lower and basic rates. Higher rate taxpayers will have an effective rate of 32.5%. This is to avoid a liability greater than that under the previous system, as illustrated by the following example:

	To 5 April 1999		From 6 April 1999	
	£		£	
UK dividend	80.00		80.00	
Tax credit	20.00	(20% of gross)	8.89	(10% of gross)
Gross Income	100.00		88.89	
Higher tax rate	40.00	(40%)	28.89	(32.5%)
After-tax income	60.00		60.00	

Dividends and interest from overseas

The tax deducted or imputed may include overseas tax as well as the UK basic rate. The latter deduction may be lower as a result of double taxation relief.

Accrued interest

From 28 February 1986, investment income for tax purposes includes accrued interest added to the price on the sale of certain securities. This would be the situation where the buyer receives a payment of interest which covers the period before the purchase. On the other hand, if the sale was made close to the date when interest was payable, the seller would receive the interest and the proportion due to the buyer would be deducted from the price. Accrued interest is chargeable to tax only where the total nominal value of the securities owned by the taxpayer is above £5,000. The securities concerned are interest-bearing securities and stock, such as government securities, local authority loans and company debentures.

Likewise manufactured dividends are taxable. These represent payments to compensate buyers of securities for loss of dividend due, for instance, to late delivery of purchased shares.

Deep gain securities

Tax is payable on the discount obtained from deep gain securities when the amount payable on the redemption of a bond exceeds the issue price by more then ½% per annum or 15% in total and when the timing and amount of the redemption is uncertain. The income tax payable reduces the capital gains tax payable on the redemption of the securities. The rules do not apply where redemption can be enforced on the default (e.g. insolvency) of the issuer.

Capital gains

For treatment of capital gains and the inheritance tax in respect of investment see Chapter 5 of this book.

3.2 PERSONAL EQUITY PLANS (PEPs)

With effect from 6 April 1999 the PEP scheme was discontinued. After 6 April 1999 an existing PEP investment can continue to be held with the same tax advantages as an ISA, but no new contributions can be made to it. Also, contrary to the initial announcement following the 1998 budget, you can change your PEP provider after this date.

After 6 April 1999, prior PEP investments can be transferred into an Individual Savings Account (ISA), without affecting the normal ISA investment limits – see 3.4 below.

For the five-year period 6 April 1999 to 5 April 2004, the tax credit on dividends from PEP shares is 10% (the same credit rate as applicable to dividends from ISA investments).

3.3 INTEREST RECEIVABLE

General

Interest receivable forms part of the total income of all taxpayers, including individuals, companies and other bodies liable to tax. In most cases income tax at 20% is deducted, or assumed to be deducted, by the payer, and this system applies with some exceptions to government securities, debentures, other quoted stock and loans generally. If the recipient of the interest is not liable to pay tax the amount deducted can be reclaimed from the Inland Revenue. From 6 April 1999, if the top band is 10%, the difference can be reclaimed. Claims for repayment of tax at £50 or over can be made before the end of the year.

Interest gross of tax

In the following cases the interest is receivable without deduction of tax:

- on National Savings accounts – see below
- from the Post Office
- on off-shore accounts, e.g. those in the Isle of Man and the Channel Islands, and when received by persons not ordinarily resident in the UK
- when application is made (on form R85) by a non-taxpayer for bank and building society interest to be paid gross. Severe penalties apply to false declarations.

Basis of assessment

Tax is now based on the amount of interest received in the tax year.

Payment of tax on interest

In most cases the taxpayer's liability for lower and basic rate tax on interest received will be satisfied by deduction of tax from the payment, the payer having to account to the Inland Revenue for the tax so deducted. Where interest is paid gross the taxpayer is liable to pay tax on the interest on 31 January in the year of assessment. However, for employees and pensioners the tax liability is usually met by the appropriate deduction from the allowances given in the coding. This adjustment to the coding is normally estimated so that a further coding adjustment may be necessary when the actual interest is known, or a refund of tax may be due.

For the purpose of calculating the taxpayer's liability to higher rate tax interest paid net of tax will be grossed up, and the excess over the basic rate will be payable on 31 January following the end of the year of assessment.

National Savings

(a) Ordinary Account. Up to £70 of interest from ordinary Savings Bank accounts is exempt from all rates of income tax.

(b) Investment Account. A higher rate of interest is payable than on the ordinary account but the interest is taxable, although tax is not deducted at source. Attractive to charities and individuals not liable to tax (who can apply for interest to be paid gross). One month's notice is required for withdrawal.

(c) National Savings Certificates and National Savings Bonds. A variety of issues have been made with tax-free interest.

(d) Save as You Earn. This is a system by which the saver contracts to make regular monthly contributions from £5 up to £150 a month to the National Savings Bank, the Trustee Savings Bank, other banks or certain building societies. A bonus, payable after certain stated periods, is tax free. At the end of three years savers have the option of taking the amount accrued in cash or buying shares in their company at a price set three years earlier, and this price can be discounted by up to 20%.

In 1995/96 ordinary save-as-you-earn contracts were abolished but tax relief continues for those linked to share options.

(e) Premium Savings Bonds. The maximum holding is £20,000 and prize money is tax-free.

(f) Government Stock on the National Savings Stock Register. The interest is paid without deduction of tax but is taxable in the recipient's hands.

(g) National Savings Pensioners Guaranteed Income Bond. The second issue of this bond is available to people aged 60 and over from 29 November 1995 and will pay monthly interest at fixed rates guaranteed for five years. Maximum holding is £1,000,000.

Tax-Exempt Special Savings Accounts (TESSA)

The TESSA scheme was discontinued with effect 6 April 1999. No new TESSA accounts could be opened after that date. However, normal subscriptions could continue over the five-year life of any TESSA opened prior to this date. In addition, any sum invested is transferable into an Individual Savings Accounts (ISA) – see 3.4 below.

TESSA accounts pay tax-free interest provided the capital is not withdrawn for five years, but the interest can be paid to the saver. The account must not be a joint account nor held on behalf of another person. After five years, the continuing interest will be taxable but no liability to tax arises when an account is withdrawn on the death of the depositor.

Savings with friendly societies

The 1994 Budget raised the maximum annual premium from £200 to £270 payable to friendly societies under tax-exempt life assurance policies. The tax-exempt surrender value is payable out of a tax-exempt fund after 10 years (or 7½ years for certain shorter-term policies) and need not be limited to a return of the premiums. These policies can represent tax-efficient forms of saving, especially for children under the age of 18.

3.4 INDIVIDUAL SAVINGS ACCOUNTS (ISAs)

This is a savings vehicle designed to make more people save. Its stated aim is to help the poor save. From 6 April 1999, it replaced new PEPs and TESSAs.

Changes have been brought in from 6 April 2005, but the main details are as follows.

- The tax benefits are guaranteed to last for at least 10 years.
- The returns are free from tax.
- There is no statutory minimum holding period or minimum subscription level.
- Qualifying investments are in 3 groups:
    - bank and building society accounts, and National Savings products
    - stocks and shares
    - life assurance.
- Normal annual subscription limit of £7,000 in total, until 2004/05, subject to:
    - maximum £3,000 in cash, until 2004/05
    - maximum £1,000 invested in life assurance
    - balance in stocks and shares, to maximum of £7,000 to 2004/05
- The existence of a PEP investment made prior to 6 April does not affect the ISA limits.
- Continuing subscription over the five-year life of a TESSA account opened prior to 6th April 1999 (see 3.2 above) will not affect the annual subscription limit to an ISA.
- Capital from a maturing TESSA can be invested in an ISA without affecting the annual subscription limit.
- For the five-year period 6 April 1999 to 5 April 2004, a 10% tax credit will be paid on dividends from UK companies in respect of shares held in either an ISA or a PEP.
- From 6 April 2001, ISAs have been available to 16/17 year olds.

Other facts:

- One company can run all aspects of the ISA (maxi) for an individual, or alternatively different companies (mini) can run the respective cash, stocks and life assurance elements separately.
- Cash can be withdrawn any time without penalty but cannot be replaced if the cash limit was already reached previously.
- No lifetime limit applies.
- Shares from de-mutualised companies cannot be bought into an ISA.
- There will not be a prize draw as suggested when the scheme was first launched.

Changes from 6 April 2005

On 6 April 2005, the ISA rules changed so that from that date:

- the separate 'mini' insurance ISA element ended and instead, depending on the type of insurance policy held, the policy qualifies for the:
    - Mini ISA cash component - with an unchanged limit of £3,000
    - Mini ISA stocks and shares component - with an increased limit of £4,000, or
    - Maxi ISA - with a limit of £7,000.

People who paid into an ISA insurance policy before 6 April 2005 can continue paying into the policy after 6 April 2005, but, if they also subscribe to a mini cash or mini stocks and shares ISA component, they may have to re-arrange their savings.

- new 'stakeholder' cash and medium-term products can be held with ISAs.

3.5 PROFIT SHARING

General

Companies operate various schemes allowing their employees, including directors, to obtain shares and share in profits in those companies on favourable terms. The employees may be offered options to acquire shares at below market prices; they may obtain the shares through Save As You Earn contracts; they may obtain interests in shares through trusts set up for the purpose; or they may be allotted shares individually. The profit-related pay schemes initiated in 1987 have now been phased out. Many conditions apply to all these schemes for tax purposes but the general effect of the legislation is outlined as follows.

Share options

Where an option is granted to a director or employee by reason of an office or employment there will generally be a charge to tax not when the option is granted, but when it is exercised. The charge will then be on the difference between the amount received and the amount paid (both for the shares and for the option itself). Liability to tax on the option can be avoided if the option is granted under one of the Inland Revenue Approved Share Option Schemes.

SAYE share option scheme

This scheme gives employees the right to buy shares at a fixed price, using the proceeds of SAYE (Save As You Earn) savings contracts. The price of the shares will be fixed at the time the option is granted, and the price must not be less than 80% of the market value of the shares at that time.

Employees do not have to use their options – this will depend on whether the shares increase in value over the period of the savings contract. If they do not use their options they will still receive the proceeds of their SAYE contract (tax free) when the contract matures.

Under the SAYE contract, the employee saves a regular amount between £10 and £250 per month for 3, 5 or 7 years. The savings will stop after the contract period, but the contract may provide for the savings, plus bonus, to be paid.

A scheme will only be approved by the Revenue if the shares used satisfy certain conditions to ensure that they are ordinary shares, and if the scheme is made available to all employees under similar terms.

If the scheme is approved the employee will not pay any income tax on:

- the granting of an option to buy shares at a favourable price
- any increase in the value of the shares between the date the option was given and the date on which it is exercised.

When the shares are sold any profit may still be charged to capital gains tax.

Company share option plans

This scheme provides similar tax reliefs to the SAYE Share Option Scheme. However, it is not linked to a savings contract, and, crucially, does not have to be operated for all employees on similar terms.

To qualify for tax reliefs, the option must be held for at least 3 and no more than 10 years, and only one option exercise can qualify for relief in any 3-year period. The scheme must also be approved by the Inland Revenue before any options are granted under it.

Only full-time directors and employees working at least 20 hours per week can participate, and there are limits on the size of options which can be granted. The maximum value of shares a person can have under option at any time is £20,000.

Profit sharing through shares

These schemes are intended to be replaced by AESOPs (see next section). No new profit sharing schemes can be registered after 6 April 2001 and no further shares can be allocated to such schemes after 1 January 2003. The object of such schemes was to provide a mechanism whereby employees would be able to obtain shares in a company without being liable to income tax on the receipt of those shares.

This scheme required the company concerned to set up a trust fund. The company then made cash payments to the trustees to buy shares in the company. The trustees then set aside some of these shares for each employee who took part in the scheme.

The scheme had to be available to all qualifying employees on similar terms. The shares could not generally be taken out of the trust for two years, and for the acquisition of the shares to be completely free of tax, the shares could not be taken out until after five years.

There were complex rules on the operation of the scheme, on the types of shares which could be used, and on the maximum amount which could be allocated to each employee.

All employee share option plans (AESOPs)

- Employers can give employees up to £3,000 of shares each year free of tax and National Insurance.

- Some or all of these shares can be awarded to employees for reaching performance targets.
- Employees will be able to buy partnership shares out of their pre-tax salary up to a maximum of £1,500 a year, free of tax and National Insurance. Employees who keep their shares in the plan for 5 years will pay no income tax or National Insurance in respect of these shares.
- If the shares are only kept in the plan for 3 years, tax and National Insurance is paid on the initial value – any increase being tax free.
- If the employees retain the shares in the plan until disposal, they will not be liable to Capital Gains Tax.
- Companies will get corporation tax relief on costs they incur in providing shares for employees to buy, to the extent that such costs exceed the employee's contributions.
- As a transitional measure, companies can run an approved profit sharing scheme alongside a new plan that provides partnership shares, although no further tax free awards will be able to be made after January 2003.
- Up to £1,500 of dividends may be reinvested in shares tax free each year within the trust.
- Employees and trustees will have freedom to make their own arrangements about transferring shares when an employee leaves.
- There is a new capital gains tax rollover relief to existing shareholders who want to sell their shares to a new plan trust to be used for the benefit of employees.
- The existence of arrangements to enable employees to sell shares in a new plan trust will not of itself make those shares readily convertible into cash, requiring the employers to operate PAYE and account for National Insurance.

Companies can send in draft plans for approval under a fast-track approvals system.

Enterprise Management Incentive Scheme

- Independent trading companies with gross assets not exceeding £15 million will be able to award key employees (prior to 5 April 2001, limited to 15 key employees) with tax advantaged share options, each receiving options worth up to £100,000 at the time of grant.
- There is no tax charge on the grant of the option and there will be normally no tax or National Insurance for the employee to pay when the options are exercised; nor will there normally be any National Insurance charge for the employer.
- From 15 May 2000, the 15 employee limit was replaced by a limit of £3 million on the total value of the shares for which there are unexercised share options. Also, the scheme is no longer limited to key employees.

When shares are sold, CGT taper relief will normally start from the date the options are granted, rather than the date they were exercised.

3.6 ENTERPRISE INVESTMENT SCHEME (EIS)

This investment scheme replaced the Business Expansion Scheme on 1 January 1994 when the latter terminated in December 1993. The main features of the scheme are as follows:

- Unquoted trading companies trading but not necessarily resident or incorporated in the UK can from 6 April 1998 raise unlimited capital by shares issued under the scheme (previously £1m per year) subject to gross assets being less than £15 million before the investment and £16 million after.

- Investors can subscribe for EIS shares up to £200,000 from 6 April 2004 (previously £150,000). This limit is available to both husband and wife.

- The investment in an EIS scheme gives tax relief at 20% and capital gains tax exemption on the first disposal of the shares. The shares must be held for three years (five years for shares issued before 6 April 2000). Half the investment made between 6 April and 5 October in any year, up to a maximum of £25,000, can be carried back to the previous tax year.

- Qualifying investors must not be employees or shareholders of the company owning more than 30% of the shares, but subsequent to the issue of the shares an investor can become a paid director, retaining the right to the tax relief.

3.7 VENTURE CAPITAL TRUSTS

VCTs provide a means whereby taxpayers can invest indirectly in unquoted shares and obtain similar tax reliefs to those available to investors in EIS shares. From 6 April 2004, individuals aged 18 or over who subscribe for new eligible shares in a VCT can claim tax relief at 40% of the amount invested up to the lower of:

    (i) the maximum investment of £200,000 (previously £100,000) per tax year, or

    (ii) the individual's tax liability for the year in which the investment takes place.

Dividends received by individuals in respect of ordinary shares in a VCT are exempt from income tax subject to certain conditions. If an individual disposees of his or her shares within three years of their issue, VCT income tax investment relief is withdrawn.

Gains arising on the disposal of VCT shares are exempt from capital gains tax up to the £200,000 investment limit in any tax year. This applies to VCT shares purchased and those acquired by subscription.

3.8 SCRIP DIVIDENDS

Where a taxpayer opts to take a dividend in the form of shares or stock, instead of cash, the dividend will be grossed up at the dividend rate of income tax (10%). The gross amount will be chargeable to the higher rate of income tax (32.5%) if applicable. The market value may apply if higher than the cash equivalent.

The capital gains tax cost of such shares is, however, the net amount, not the grossed up equivalent.

3.9 UNIT TRUSTS

Authorised unit trusts and investment trusts are exempt from capital gains tax after 31 January 1980. In the case of those trusts with specific instructions as to their operations, income from investment in gilt-edged stock is liable to basic rate income tax and not corporation tax. In both cases the holder will be liable to capital gains tax on the disposal of his or her holding, subject to normal exemptions. Regulations under the Charities Act 1992, effective on 1 January 1993, enable charitable unit trusts to transmit income to participating charities without deduction of tax.

When authorised under company law, open-ended investment companies (OEIC) will fall under the same provisions as apply to unit trusts. Open-ended investment companies are those where their shares are continuously created or redeemed.

3.10 OFFSHORE FUNDS

The offshore funds legislation applies to a wide range of investment vehicles set up overseas, often in the form of open-ended investment companies or unit trusts. If a significant proportion of the income is distributed to investors, the capital gains on the disposal of the investment is liable to capital gains tax. Where capital gains are rolled up in the fund the investors are charged income tax on the disposal of their holdings.

4

Business Taxation

4.1 THE SYSTEM SUMMARISED

The assessment

The profits from trading and professional activities are assessed as a separate source of income.

In strictness, none of the personal reliefs and allowances reviewed in the previous chapters of this book is applicable to a business assessment as such. But where the business is unincorporated, i.e. owned by one person or a partnership, the reliefs and allowances applicable to the owners may be set off against their share of the business assessment. A limited company is, however, a 'legal person' and the tax assessment made on its own profits is not subject to the reliefs due to the owners, that is the shareholders, even if it is effectively owned by one person.

Unincorporated businesses

The profits of a business owned by one individual or a partnership are liable to income tax. The amount so payable may be reduced by the owners' reliefs and allowances. It may be, however, that all of an individual taxpayer's reliefs are set off against income other than the profits from his or her business, and this situation should normally occur where the taxpayer was in a salaried employment as well as running a business. In the case of a partnership a return of the partnership computation must be made on behalf of the firm and the individual partners must make returns of their own incomes, including that received from the partnership. The tax payable is due by the individual partners in the agreed profit-sharing ratios.

Incorporated businesses

So far as most limited companies and many other corporate bodies are concerned, their taxable profits are subject to corporation tax and not income tax.

Funds must be kept available for the payment of the tax liability nine months after the company's year end.

The dividend in the hands of the shareholder comes with a non-refundable tax credit at 10%.

Whether the business is incorporated or not the profits which it shows in its accounts will almost always need adjustment for the purpose of arriving at the profit figure on which tax is payable. This aspect of the subject is considered in the next section.

4.2 ADJUSTING THE ACCOUNTS PROFIT

General – the basis of adjustment

The profit shown in the accounts of a business, whether it is incorporated or not, is adjusted for tax purposes (a) by adding back expenses disallowed, and (b) by deducting income which is not taxable. The resulting assessment may then be reduced by capital allowances, and loss relief. The question as to whether a particular item is allowable or not is sometimes difficult to determine, and is a frequent cause of appeal to the Commissioners and to the Courts. For profits arising from trading, the over-riding rules are that expenditure must (a) be wholly and exclusively incurred for the purpose of the trade or profession, and (b) not be of a capital nature.

Recent announcements both in the 2001 Budget and elsewhere indicate that the government is moving (slowly) to accepting accounting figures as being those used for tax purposes.

Expenses disallowed

The following expenses are not allowed in the tax computation – that is, they must be added back to the accounts profits or deducted from an accounts loss:

- Expenses not arising out of the trade or profession, e.g. medical fees.
- Withdrawals of capital and profits, e.g. by dividends, proprietors' or partners' shares of profit or salaries (but salaries payable to directors of limited companies are normally allowable).
- Capital expenditure, such as extensions or improvements to premises, legal expenses connected with capital expenditure, company formation expenses, and capital losses (but see also under Capital Gains).
- Depreciation. Capital allowances (see below) may be available in place of depreciation.
- Personal expenditure of proprietors such as personal life insurance premiums and private usage of business cars.
- Annual payments from which tax has been deducted, where the business is unincorporated and pays income tax.
- Appropriations of profit such as dividends, reserves and taxation.
- General provisions for bad debts, e.g. by applying a percentage, but reasonable provisions against specific debtors and actual bad debts are allowed.
- Entertainment expenses and gifts. Relief for entertainment of foreign customers was abolished in 1988/89. However, the general rule is relaxed for gifts to

employees and gifts to any one person in a year costing no more than £50 with a conspicuous advertisement and which are not food, drink, tobacco or gift vouchers.

- Cost of appealing against income tax assessments; and accountants' fees in connection with an Inland Revenue investigation, unless there is no alteration to the Tax Return under enquiry, in which case most, if not all, the accountants' fees are allowable.
- Penalties for breaches of the law.
- Deductions for self-cancelling annuities representing tax avoidance schemes were not allowable (Moodie v IRC 1993 HL following W. T. Ramsey v CIR 1982, AC).

Allowable expenses

In general, business expenses which do not fall under the foregoing prohibitions are allowable for tax purposes but the following allowable expenses are worthy of special mention:

- Repairs and maintenance of trade premises, plant, fittings, vehicles, etc., not being of the nature of additions or improvements. Renewals are not allowed if capital allowances are claimed.
- Rent and rates of trade or professional premises. Where part of a private residence is exclusively used for the business a proportion of the rent and a proportion of any premium may be claimed. This proportion may be based on floor area.
- Employees' remuneration, directors' fees, employer's National Insurance contributions and contributions to approved superannuation funds payable by the business. The self-employed cannot charge their own National Insurance contributions against their profits.
- Business insurance premiums, but sums received under claims must be brought into account as well as the expense.
- Travelling expenses wholly and exclusively incurred for the purpose of the business, but note that employees earning £8,500 and directors may have to justify reimbursed expenses and expense allowances. Travelling expenses include reasonable hotel expenses necessarily incurred.
- Losses from theft, but see under insurance above.
- Advertising, if not of a capital nature.
- Dilapidations payable on terminations of leases to the extent that the payment represents deferred repairs.
- Losses on exchange as they accrue if clearly a risk of the trade. Consideration will be given to allowing, or treating as income, exchange differences on monetary assets and, from 6 April 1993, these differences are not subject to capital gains tax.

- Compensation to employees arising out of their terms of service; also voluntary pensions and gratuities on retirement. Redundancy payments and additions thereto up to three times the amount of the redundancy payment.
- Bank interest payable by limited companies, provided it is a proper business expense. Interest paid by the self-employed may have to be apportioned between business and private use.
- The incidental costs of obtaining loans or issuing loan stock.
- Pre-trading expenditure for trades, professions, etc. Businesses beginning trading on and after 1 April 1993 may claim relief for expenditure incurred up to the previous seven years.
- Salaries of staff lent to charities and approved educational establishments.
- Discount and incidental costs of issuing bills of exchange accepted by banks.
- Employees' expenses on approved retraining courses, including sandwich courses, within the UK and for up to a year. The expenses include lodging, subsistence, books and travelling. The employee must have two years' service with the employer; the facility must be available to all employees of a similar class; and the course must start during employment or two years thereafter.
- Gifts of equipment to schools and other educational establishments, and other charitable gifts.
- The cost of setting up employee share schemes and AESOPs.
- Accountancy expenses in preparing accounts and negotiating routine tax liabilities, but not those for Inland Revenue investigations which reveal that profits have not been fully declared.
- Cost of food and a proportion of business accommodation when working away from home (Prior v Saunders 1993).

Assessable income

Fewer problems arise with regard to the income or credit side of the profit and loss account of a business. The major part of business income in the form of sales to customers or fees charged to clients needs no adjustment for tax purposes. The following, however, merit particular mention:

- Capital profits on the sale of fixed assets will affect capital allowances and may be subject to the capital gains tax provisions, but are not otherwise taxable.
- Casual profits are normally assessable either as trading income or other income.
- Exchange profits will be assessable if arising out of the trade carried on.
- Profits from illegal trading are assessable.
- Rent receivable from unfurnished letting is normally assessable as it accrues.
- Grants received, except where the grant is for capital expenditure or compensation for loss of capital assets.

Income not assessable

Some part of the income shown in the accounts of businesses may not be assessable for income tax or corporation tax. This will usually be the case where the income is not derived from the trade carried on or where it is of a capital nature. In the case of income not derived from the trade under assessment it is, however, possible that the Inspector of Taxes may take the view that a new trade has been established and make an assessment on those grounds. Where income is of a capital nature – for example, a profit on the sale of plant – that profit may be subject to the capital gains provisions if the proceeds exceed the original cost of the plant. Other examples of non-assessable income are as follows:

- Gifts received are not normally assessable, unless they consist of benefits to directors and higher-paid employees, and exceed £100 in a year.
- Damages receivable in a legal action are of a capital nature, and so is compensation, e.g. on cancellation of an agreement.
- Regional development grants.

PAYE and National Savings contributions

The amounts deducted from the remuneration of employees, including national insurance, are normally refunded to the Inland Revenue monthly. The payments, including National Insurance, can be made quarterly if they average less than £1,500 per month.

4.3 A SPECIMEN COMPUTATION

The following specimen computation of a fictitious business is intended to illustrate a selection of the points mentioned above. For simplicity the accounts of a partnership business are used as certain special considerations which are dealt with later apply to limited companies. Essentially, however, the method is the same whatever the form of the business concerned.

A and B in partnership
TRADING AND PROFIT AND LOSS ACCOUNT
for the year ended 31 December 2004

	£	£	£
Sales, less returns and VAT			200,000
Less: cost of goods sold			120,000
GROSS PROFIT			80,000
Less: operating expenses			
Salaries:	£	£	
Partners	20,000		
Staff	18,000		
Total salaries		38,000	
National Insurance:			
Partners	2,200		
Staff	1,800		
Total Nat. Insurance		4,000	
Rent and rates	2,000		
Maintenance and improvement			
of premises	1,000		
Total premises expense		3,000	
Insurance:			
General	700		
Partners' life insurance	300		
Total insurance		1,000	
Travelling:			
Fares	300		
Subsistence	200		
Car expenses, incl. petrol,			
oil, depreciation & repairs	2,500		
Total travelling		3,000	
Entertainment		200	
Stationery & postage		400	
Advertising		800	
Donations & subscriptions:			
Local hospital	50		
Golf club	150		

71

Total donations	200	
Bad debts written off	300	
Provision for doubtful debts		
at 5% of debtors	1,200	
Depreciation of equipment	1,900	
Total operating expenses		54,000
Operating profit		£26,000
Add: Non-trading income:		
Insurance commission	150	
Profit on sale of van	350	
Total non-trading income		500
		26,500
Less: Non-trading expenses:		
Interest on loan, gross	1,420	
Interest on partners' capital	580	
Total non-trading expenses		2,000
PRETAX PROFIT		24,500
Less: Income tax provision		6,500
NET PROFIT AFTER TAX		£18,000

TAX COMPUTATION BASED ON THE ABOVE ACCOUNTS

	£	£	Comments
Profits per accounts before tax		24,500	● Income tax is an appropriation of profit
Add back charges disallowed:			
Partners' salaries	20,000		● Regarded as appropriation of profit; directors' salaries would normally be allowed if the business was a limited company.
Partners' Nat. Insurance	2,200		

Improvements to premises	500	● A capital expense
Car expenses	130	● Disallowed for private use – see text for details of method
Partners' life assurance	300	● A personal expense
Entertainment	200	● Disallowable expenses
Golf club subscription	150	● Probably not wholly and necessarily expended for business purposes; the amount for the local hospital may be allowed.
Provision for doubtful debts	1,200	● Only the write-off against specific debts is allowable.
Depreciation	1,900	● Capital allowances are available instead.
Interest on loan	1,420	● Possibly subject to deduction of tax at source.
Interest on partners' capital	580	● An appropriation of profit.
	28,580	
	53,080	
Deduct income not chargeable:		
Profit on sale of van	350	● Capital – will affect capital allowances
Adjusted profit	£52,730	

The adjusted profit would be reduced by capital allowances and loss relief to arrive at taxable profits, and would be apportioned to the partners in their profit-sharing ratios. The amount so apportioned would then form part of each partner's personal computation.

Rounding of business computations

Subject to some qualifications, the Inland Revenue are prepared to accept business computations of profits rounded to the nearest £1,000. This applies where such rounding is applied to the business accounts and turnover is not less than £5 million. In particular rounding does not apply to: chargeable gains (except for incidental costs of acquisition and disposal); tax credit relief for overseas companies; accrued income and most computations of capital allowances.

4.4 CAPITAL ALLOWANCES

Meaning and purpose of 'capital allowances'

The figure for the depreciation of fixed assets which is charged in the accounts of a business is not allowable for tax purposes. Instead of depreciation various 'capital allowances' may be deducted from the assessed profits. Many people are confused as to why depreciation is not allowed but capital allowances are. The depreciation figure in the accounts is an accounting adjustment calculated to progressively write off the assets over their useful lives (producing a "fair and reasonable" representation of the actual value of the Company's assets). Capital allowances represent the amount of write-off which is allowed for tax purposes – normally greater than the depreciation amount for the first few years, particularly in the first year. The (faster) rate at which an asset can be written down for tax purposes bears no relation to the actual value or life of the assets concerned; it is a governmental concession designed to stimulate capital investment by offering the carrot of higher tax relief in the year of purchase. In effect the tax reliefs are all skewed towards the front end of the asset life, so that instead of having an even progression of tax reliefs, they are mostly taken in the early years, resulting in lower tax in those earlier years and correspondingly higher tax in later years. For the purpose of the accounts, the assets are recorded at their fair value, not their artificially low "tax-written-down" value, and the amount of tax initially saved (or, in effect, deferred) as a result of the accelerated write-down is recorded in the accounts as "deferred tax".

Capital allowances apply to industrial buildings, ships, mines, oil wells, plant and machinery. The term 'plant and machinery' covers a wide field and includes vehicles, furniture, fixtures and fittings for business purposes.

Capital allowances are applicable only to plant and machinery belonging to the trader, but the payment of a deposit indicates ownership. If the expenditure becomes abortive, disposal value will apply.

There are essentially four groups of capital allowances: first-year allowances, initial allowances, writing-down allowances (formerly known as 'annual allowances' or 'wear and tear allowances') and balancing allowances or balancing charges.

First-year allowances

These allowances apply to plant and machinery (defined widely) and represent a percentage of the cost when the expenditure was incurred and the asset acquired. The March 2000 budget made a first year allowance of 40% permanent. The rate of first-year allowances incurred on most plant and machinery by small businesses has been increased to 50% (from 40%) for a period of one year. For income tax purposes, the increased rate will apply to expenditure incurred on or after 6 April 2004, and for corporation tax purposes, it will apply to expenditure incurred on or after 1 April 2004. The rate of first-year allowances for medium sized businesses remains unchanged at 40%. It is available to businesses defined as small and medium (See below.) Capital expenditure on research and development (not including buildings) qualifies for an allowance, 100% of cost.

Small businesses that invested in Information and Communications Technology equipment (computers, software and internet-enabled mobile phones) over 4 years from 1 April 2000 to 31 March 2004, could claim 100% first year allowances. A business was small if it satisfied at least two of the following criteria:

- turnover less than £2.8 million
- assets less than £1.4 million
- not more than 50 employees.

The first-year allowances were only available to small and/or medium-sized businesses as defined as satisfying 2 of the 3 following conditions for the current or previous year (current year only in the case of companies) with:

- turnover less than £11.2 million
- assets less than £5.6 million
- not more than 250 employees.

A new business premises renovation allowance scheme will provide 100 percent first year capital allowance for capital expenditure incurred in renovating or converting property that has been vacant for year or more in one of the designated disadvantaged areas. The scheme will apply to individuals or companies who own or lease the property once state aid approval has been granted.

The allowances do not apply to expenditure on machinery and plant for leasing or letting on hire, cars, long-life assets, sea-going ships and railway assets. These must rely on the standard 'writing-down allowances' referred to below.

After the first-year allowance has been taken, where applicable, subsequent write-down allowances are provided by 'writing-down allowances' for the following years (see below).

Landlord's energy saving allowance

A new allowance has been introduced for landlords who incur capital expenditure on installing loft or cavity wall insulation in a dwelling house which they let on or after 6 April 2004. The new rules will provide for a tax deduction on such expenditure up to a maximum of £1,500. The new rules will apply for income tax purposes only.

Initial allowances

Initial allowances were calculated on cost and were additional to writing-down allowances (see below) also calculated on cost in the first year. They applied generally to expenditure on industrial and commercial buildings but, subject to the exceptions indicated below, were abolished for expenditure after 31 March 1986. The cases where the allowances continue to apply include expenditure on industrial and commercial buildings, including shops and offices, in Enterprise Zones. The allowance is 100% of cost including VAT unless a writing-down allowance of 25% on cost is claimed instead.

Writing-down allowances

(a) Plant and machinery. The standard writing-down allowance on plant and machinery is 25%. Expenditure on or after 26 November 1996 on assets with a working life of at least 25 years ('long-life' assets) qualifies for a writing-down allowance of 6% per annum where the total expenditure on such assets exceeds £100,000 in any tax year. Expenditure of less than £100,000 on long-life assets during a tax year will qualify for a writing-down allowance of 25%.

The writing-down allowance is an annual allowance calculated on the balance of a "pool" of the cost or written-down values of all applicable assets. There is a pool for plant and machinery generally and business cars (used for business only) costing less than £12,000. A balance brought forward on the existing pool is added to the main pool. Cars with any element of private use have to be treated separately as referred to below. The maximum writing-down allowance on individual cars costing over £12,000 is £3,000 p.a. The balance in the pool is increased by the cost of assets purchased and decreased by the proceeds from any assets sold as well as by the writing-down allowance for each year. The 1986 Finance Act included provisions for depooling of shorter-life assets, other than cars or ships, with lives of up to four years and acquired on or after 1 April 1986.

Example

	FYA	Pool	Claim
	£	£	£
WDA b/fwd		10,000	
Additions qualifying for FYA	4,000		
FYA (40%)	(1,600)		1,600
	2,400		
Sale proceeds		(2,000)	
		8,000	
WDA 25%		(2,000)	2,000
		6,000	
Transfer to pool	(2,400)	2,400	
	-		
WDA C/fwd		8,400	
Total capital allowance claimed in year			3,600

Where assets are fully written off by the 100% first-year allowance they are obviously not eligible for any writing-down allowance in addition. For assets not subject to the first-year allowance the writing-down allowance can be claimed in the year of purchase. In all instances, these allowances are the maximum claimable. The taxpayer can 'disclaim' or reduce the amount claimed, if a full claim would not attract any tax relief due to the taxable income falling below the personal allowance.

Example: using the capital allowance example above.

	£
Profits (as adjusted for tax purposes)	7,000
Less capital allowance (1,600 + 2,000)	3,600
Statutory Total income	3,400
Less personal allowance	4,615
'Wasted' capital allowance	£(1,215)

The taxpayer could disclaim £1,215 of the above writing down allowances. It is often wiser to claim first year allowances when available and disclaim the writing down allowance. The higher first year allowances are by their nature only available in the first year.

Amending the above allowance computation:

	FYA £	Pool £	Claim £
WDA b/fwd		10,000	
Additions qualifying for FYA	4,000		
FYA (40%)	(1,600)		1,600
	2,400		
Sale proceeds		(2,000)	
		8,000	
WDA (restricted)		(785)	785
		7,215	
Transfer to pool	(2,400)	2,400	
	—		
WDA c/fwd		9,615	
Total capital allowance claimed in year			2,385

	£
Adjusted profits	7,000
Less: capital allowance	(2,385)
Statutory Total Income	4,615
Less: personal allowance	(4,615)
Taxable income	—

(b) Industrial buildings, agricultural buildings and hotels. The writing-down allowance is 4% applied each year to the cost, including the first year, and is deducted from the written-down balance as well as the first-year allowance, where applicable. To qualify for the allowance a hotel must have at least 10 bedrooms, be open to the public for at least four months in a year and provide breakfast and an evening meal as part of the normal service. Where industrial buildings are leased for over 50 years the lessee can claim the allowance provided there is a joint election by both lessor and lessee.

The rate of writing-down allowance for agricultural buildings is also 4% from 1 April 1986. From 1 April 1986, a system of balancing adjustments operates at the taxpayer's option when a building is demolished or sold. In 1982/83 the allowance was extended to include buildings used for certain repairing and servicing activities. For expenditure after 19 June 1989, the agricultural buildings allowance no longer applies to forestry land.

From 6 April 1995 capital allowances could be claimed for private investment in public roads, including toll roads.

From 11 May 2001, 100% capital allowances are available for property owners or occupiers to claim 'up-front' tax relief on providing flats for rent. This is for expenditure on the renovation or conversion of vacant or underused space above shops or commercial premises built before 1980 in traditional shopping areas.

(c) Private cars used for business. These have to be accounted for individually (not in a pool), and a writing-down allowance of 25% is allowable on each vehicle, each year. The amount of the allowance which is set off against tax will depend on the proportion of business/private use. The maximum claimable per car per annum before splitting between private and business is £3,000. For a new car registered between 17 April 2002 and 31 March 2008, emitting up to 120 g/km, or electrically propelled, 100% first-year allowances are available.

Balancing allowances and balancing charges

These allowances or charges apply in the year when the asset is sold or scrapped and their purpose is to ensure that no more nor less than the net cost of an asset, after deducting receipts from the eventual sale, is allowable as a charge against taxable profits. Where the pool system is in use the sale proceeds are deducted from the balance in the pool. If the sale proceeds are greater than the pool balance, the difference is a balancing charge, i.e. added to profit. If the sale proceeds exceed the cost, then a capital gain may arise on that excess. With the pool system balancing allowances normally arise only on cessation of a business but they may arise for 'depooled' short life assets. In addition items which have their own pool such as cars (greater than £12,000 cost) and assets with a proportion of private use will certainly lead to a balancing adjustment, unless disposed at written-down value.

Basis period

Capital allowances refer to the accounting year on which the assessment is based. The profits of a business in single ownership or a partnership would, for the accounts year to, say, 31 December 2003, normally be assessed for the tax year 2003/04. Capital allowances to be deducted from the assessment would refer to assets acquired in the year to 31 December 2003. But see also under section 4.6 below.

Replaced plant

Where a balancing charge arises on the disposal of an asset which is to be replaced, the taxpayer can elect to deduct the balancing charge from the cost of the new asset, but this would reduce allowances on the latter.

Leased plant

In general, first year allowances are not available for expenditure on plant and machinery for leasing or letting on hire. A writing down allowance of 25% can be claimed by trading lessors on plant obtained for leasing.

Following the decision in the case of Baldwin Industrial Services Plc and Barr Ltd, the Inland Revenue have accepted that the supply of plant and machinery with an operator, by a business, is the provision of a service and not merely hire. Such plant and equipment does, therefore, qualify for first-year allowances providing the business meets all other criteria for claiming first-year allowances.

Income tax losses due to capital allowances and arising from leasing are not available for set-off against non-leasing income by individuals or partnerships, except a full-time leasing business carried on for at least six months.

The budget in March 2000 introduced a new rule which enables allowances to be claimed by the lessor on the lower of cost to and sale by the lessee, provided certain conditions are met:

a) the equipment is new when acquired by the lessee

b) the acquisition is not from a connected person, a sale and lease back or a 'main benefit' sale

c) the equipment is sold to the lessor not more than 4 months after it is first brought into use and the lessee does not claim capital allowance.

Leased cars

Taxis, private hire cars and those hired out for short terms, or to disabled persons, qualify for writing-down allowances of 25% in the year of acquisition, with a limit to the cost of £12,000. Short term means hiring for no more than 30 days to a particular person, and for less than 90 days in 12 months.

The lessee can charge the whole cost of the rental for the car (assuming it is used for business purposes) provided the retail price was no more that £12,000. Where the retail price exceeds £12,000 the allowable charge in the lessee's computation is that proportion of the rental which is represented by the following fraction: £12,000 plus half the excess price over £12,000 divided by the price.

Hire purchase

The business which obtains plant by means of hire purchase may claim capital allowances on all capital expenditure (excluding the interest charge) incurred under the contract as though it had been incurred when the contract began.

Security assets

From 5 April 1989, expenditure by individuals or partnerships on business are eligible for capital allowances. These are assets provided to meet a special threat to an individual's security, but exclude cars, ships, aircraft and living accommodation.

Enterprise Zones

The Enterprise Zones scheme began in 1980 to encourage business in certain areas but further expansion of the scheme ceased in 1987. The scheme provides an initial allowance of 100% of expenditure on the construction, improvement or extension of industrial and commercial buildings in the zone. Alternatively a 25% straight-line annual writing-down allowance can be claimed. The construction must be incurred within ten years of the designation of an area as an Enterprise Zone, and also applies to expenditure incurred within ten years thereafter under a contract made within the original ten-year period. If the building was sold before being put into use the purchaser would receive the allowance, and would do so if the building was acquired within two years of being brought into use.

Films, discs and tapes

Expenditure on the production or acquisition of the original master version of a film, disc or tape (not reproductions) is regarded as revenue expenditure for tax purposes. Income from the exploitation of the film or master negatives is likewise regarded as of a revenue, not capital nature. The amount of the expenditure which can be written off in a period of account is divided either by the 'income matching method' or the 'cost recovery method'. By the first method the expenditure to be written off in a period of account is related to the proportion of the total estimated income received in that period, subsequent adjustments becoming necessary when total income is revised. The cost recovery method provides that, by a claim within two years of the end of a period of account, total expenditure in a period exactly equals the value realised.

Energy efficient plant and machinery

100% first year allowances are also available for expenditure in accounting periods ending on or after 6 April 2001 on new plant and machinery that meets certain energy efficiency criteria.

Enhanced Capital Allowances

Expenditure incurred by businesses on or after 1 April 2003 on specified plant or machinery which meets strict water saving or efficiency criteria will qualify for 100% first-year allowances. Details of the qualifying plant and machinery are to be made available on the internet at **www.eca.gov.uk.**

4.5 TURNOVER UNDER £15,000

The Inland Revenue accepts simplified (3-line) accounts where the turnover is less than £15,000. This information is entered on the Self-Assessment tax return. The Accounts themselves need not be submitted as well.

The arrangement applies to individuals and partnerships, including those receiving rental income below the limit. These simplified accounts are limited to a statement of turnover less the total of the business expenses arrived at in accordance with the tax rules indicated above. Details of capital allowances claimed must also be stated on the return., and included in the expenses figure. The Tax Inspector may, however, call for further information, possibly full accounts, especially if a loss is shown or the business is subdivided so that each unit falls below the turnover limit. For these reasons, as well as for internal management purposes, it is always desirable for a small venture to have full accounts prepared and available.

4.6 UNINCORPORATED BUSINESSES/PARTNERSHIPS

Basis of assessment

Assessment is made on a 'current year basis', based on profits in the accounting year ending in the tax year of assessment.

Returns of partnership income are made by a 'representative partner' and assessed on the partnership. Individual partners are required to self-assess their total income, including that from the partnership.

Cessation

Certain trading expenses are eligible for tax relief after a business ceases and can be set off against the income and/or capital gains of the individual who pays such expenses. The expenditure concerned could include that which was closely related to the former business or professional activities such as: the cost of remedying defective work, insurance premiums and legal costs in connection with defective work, debts which have become bad debts after the cessation of the business and the costs of debt collection. No relief will be given where these expenses have been charged (e.g. by way of provisions) on the business accounts. The expenditure must be incurred within 7 years after the trade ceases and claims must be made within 2 years after the year of assessment in which the expense is paid.

Change of Partners

Where one or more members of a partnership leave the firm, and where new partners are introduced, the old partnership is theoretically discontinued and a new partnership is assumed to be set up. If at least one of the old partners remains, an election can be made for tax purposes within two years of the change to treat the firm as a continuing business.

Stock valuation on cessation

The valuation of stock when a business is sold or discontinued and transferred to a connected person must be as for an arm's-length transaction.

4.7 RELIEF FOR LOSSES

Basically, there are three ways of dealing with a business loss (which means a taxable loss after adjusting the accounts in the manner set out above).

Carry forward

The first method, which applies to both unincorporated businesses and to limited companies, is to carry forward the loss and set it off against the next available profits from the same trade. If the next trading profits are insufficient to absorb the whole of the loss then the balance is carried forward to be set off against the following assessment and so on. There is no time limit except for 'hobby farmers', where the limit is six years. Capital allowances which cannot be deducted from an assessment because a loss has been incurred may also be carried forward indefinitely until they can be set off against profits. In effect, therefore, capital allowances increase the loss.

Carry back of losses in the first three years of trading

A second method is to 'carry back' the losses. For an unincorporated business or partnership, where a loss occurred in any of the first three years of trading, that loss can be set off against profits or an individual's general income of the preceding three years, absorbing income of the earliest year first. For an incorporated business (i.e. a limited company) business losses can be carried back for one year and set off against the company's earlier profits.

Set-off against total income

A third method of dealing with a business loss, which applies only to individuals and unincorporated businesses or partnerships, is to offset the loss incurred by an individual in business against the total statutory income for the year of assessment in which the loss was incurred or the preceding year. If the total statutory income of a taxpayer for 2003/04 was £10,000 and he or she sustained a loss in the business of £1,700 for the financial year to 31 March 2004, the taxpayer could claim to have the £1,700 set off against the £10,000 and thus reduce the 2003/04 assessment to £8,300 or alternatively, against total statutory income of the preceding year. A claim will be admitted only where the business which sustains the loss is carried on with a reasonable expectation of profit.

Capital gains

Where trading losses are set off against statutory total income of a given year and there still remain excess losses, S72 FA1991 permits a taxpayer to offset such excess losses against capital gains for the year after deducting current year or brought forward capital losses. In such cases, the taxpayer cannot specify the amount of the claim and so the annual exempt amount may be fully or partly wasted.

4.8 COMPANIES AND CORPORATION TAX

Limited company

Limited companies and other corporate bodies are assessed for corporation tax on the profits, adjusted for tax purposes, made in the company's accounting year.

Scope and nature of the tax

Limited companies as well as most other corporate bodies and some trading clubs and unincorporated associations are liable to pay corporation tax, but not income tax, on their profits as adjusted for tax purposes. Unincorporated businesses, owned by individuals or partnerships, are assessed for income tax. Dividends paid by companies do not reduce the profit assessable to corporation tax.

Advance Corporation Tax ceased to apply from 6 April 1999. Companies are required to pay all the Corporation Tax due within nine months of their year end.

Rates of tax

The rates of corporation tax are:

(a) for **small companies** – small companies are those with profits (including dividends received plus the tax credit) up to £300,000.

Profits £	Corporation tax 2004/05 and 2005/06
0-10,000	Starting rate zero
10,001-50,000	Marginal relief 19/400
50,001-300,000	Small companies rate 19%
300,001-1,500,000	Marginal relief 11/400
1,500,001 or more	Main rate 30%

The Government has made the extraction of profits by way of dividend in small companies less attractive with effect from 1 April 2004. After this date, a minimum rate of 19% corporation tax will apply where a company whose profits are below the threshold for the small companies' rate, distributes profits to a non-company shareholder.

Where a company has one or more associated companies, the limits are divided by the number of companies involved. A company is associated where one company controls another, or companies are under common control.

Examples: 2005/06

1. Profits up to £10,000   = nil payable, if not distributed (£1,900 if distributed to non-company shareholders)
2. Profits £50,000 @ 19%   = £9,500 payable
3. Profits £20,000 (undistributed)
   – first £10 000 @ 0%   = nil
   – second £10,000 @ 23.5%   = £2,350

(b) for **large companies**, 30% in 2005/06 (30% also in 2004/05).

Where profits are above the small company limit of £300,000 and up to £1,500,000, marginal relief applies. The marginal relief consists of the large company rate on the profits, less 11/400 of the amount by which the profits fall short of the upper limit. Thus, if in 2003/04, profits were £500,000, the corporation tax would be:

		£
	30% on £500,000	150,000
Less:	$\frac{11}{400}$ x (1,500,000 – £500,000)	27,500
		122,500

In this case the corporation tax payable of £122,500 represents an effective rate of 24.5% on the profits.

The basis of assessment

Limited companies are assessed to corporation tax on their taxable profits, less capital allowances, for each accounting period. The taxable profits include profits from all sources, including capital gains but excluding dividends received from other UK companies. Corporation tax applies to the year beginning 1 April. Payment is due nine months after the end of the accounting period.

Large companies with taxable profits of £1.5 million p.a. or more (around 20,000 in number) moved to paying corporation tax in quarterly instalments for accounting periods ending on or after 1 July 1999. This new system was brought in over 4 years.

Computation of profit

The general rule is that a computation for corporation tax purposes is based on income tax principles and is made under the appropriate Schedules and Cases as apply to an income tax computation. The whole of the sources of income which falls under the various Schedules and Cases is, however, aggregated so that a single total is arrived at on which corporation tax is payable. The same rules as for income tax decide what income is assessable or not and what charges are allowable or not; but there are certain exceptions as explained below.

Corporation tax is chargeable on all income, however arising. Income from trading overseas is assessed whether actually received or not but overseas taxation is allowed as a deduction against such income. Dividends received from UK companies are not chargeable to corporation tax.

Capital gains (see later section) are treated as part of profits for the purpose of corporation tax and therefore chargeable at the appropriate corporation tax rate.

Yearly interest and other annual payments are deductible for corporation tax purposes and the system of capital allowances applies. Losses may be carried forward. Trading losses may be set off against other income of the same period or of preceding periods. Dividends or other forms of distribution of profit do not constitute charges against income. Under the Gift Aid Scheme, UK resident companies may obtain relief for one-off payments to charity by treating this payment as a charge against income. From April 2000, payments are made gross.

From April 2000, payments by companies under charitable covenants are relieved as Gift Aid payments, and paid gross. Prior to this date, payments under charitable covenants were relieved a as charge provided basic rate tax was deducted from the payment.

A specimen computation

The profit and loss account for a company for the year ended 31 March 2005 might show the following figures.

	£	£
Trading profit, adjusted for tax		2,770,000
Interest on government stock		
received 31.12.04, gross	10,000	
Dividends from UK companies,		
received 1.5.04, net	7,200	
		17,200
		2,787,200
Less: Debenture interest paid, on 31.12.04 gross		80,000
		2,707,200
Less: Dividends paid 1.6.04		36,600
		2,670,600

Capital gains for the year were £100,000; loss relief brought forward was £50,000; and capital allowances were £50,000. There are several associated companies, so no marginal small company relief is due.

The computation for corporation tax was as follows:

	£
Trading profit	2,770,000
Add: Interest received	10,000
	2,780,000
Less: Debenture interest	80,000
	2,700,000
Add: Capital gains	100,000
	2,800,000
Less: Capital allowances	50,000
	2,750,000
Less: Loss relief	50,000
Profits chargeable to Corporation Tax	2,700,000
Mainstream corporation tax at 30%:	810,000

Groups of companies

A loss incurred by a company which is a member of a group may be set off against the profit made by another member of the group. The test of group membership is ownership of 75% of the ordinary shares. The right to carry forward a tax loss is restricted where a change in the ownership of a company is associated with a change in the nature of its trade.

4.9 INVESTMENT COMPANIES AND CLOSE COMPANIES

General

An investment company is one whose main purpose is to make and obtain income from investments. These include companies formed for the purpose of administering family investments in securities and land; but there are many large investment companies. The taxable profits of these companies (as well as those of insurance companies) are assessed after deducting 'management expenses' (s 75 Taxes Act 1988), which are essentially the expenses of managing the company.

Excess management expenses and charges (such as interest payments) cannot be claimed where, during a three-year period, the ownership of an investment company changes, the business has become small or negligible and is revived after the change, or there is a significant increase in capital three years after the change or before the change.

Close companies

A close company is one which does not have a quotation on a stock exchange and of which less than 35% of the shares are held by the public. More specifically it is one controlled by five or fewer 'participators' and their associates, of which all partners and near relatives are treated as one individual for the purpose. Close investment companies are liable for corporation tax at 30% on profits. The small companies' rate does not apply to these companies, nor the starting rate.

A close company making a loan to a participator used to be liable to tax on the amount of the loan, within 14 days after the end of the accounting period. This provision extended to directors' overdrawn current accounts. This provision proved to be virtually impossible to operate as very few companies could establish the figures within 14 days of the year end. Accordingly, in the 1995 Budget this period was extended to 9 months for accounting periods ending on or after 31 March 1996. In addition, no tax is to be paid if the 'loan' is repaid within this 9 months. If it is repaid after this 9-month period, the tax is paid a year later.

4.10 BUSINESS EXPANSION SCHEME

In essence the regulations gave relief of income tax to individuals for investment in the ordinary shares of new companies carrying on new trades or intending to do so within four months of the issue of the shares. The relief consisted of the amount invested in the shares but was reduced by any amount received on the shares, e.g. by way of repayment or sale, within five years of their issue. This relief was particularly valuable to someone paying higher rate tax. The scheme was terminated at the end of December 1993 and was replaced by the Enterprise Investment scheme – see Section 3.7.

4.11 SELF-EMPLOYED PERSONS

A. Employed or self-employed?

The Income Tax (Earnings and Pensions) Act 2003 basically applies to persons who work for wages or salaries under a contract of employment. The Income Tax (Trading and Other Income) Act 2005 Part 2 applies to persons or partners operating a separate business. Apart from remuneration, the advantages of being employed under a contract of service include possible inclusion in the employer's pension scheme, redundancy pay, maternity pay and other business and social security benefits. On the other hand a person operating his or her own business receives more tax allowances for business expenses, but has to pay for pensions, and must, of course, provide capital and accept risk. To decide whether you are employed or self-employed for tax purposes, try the following questions.

Employed

If you can answer 'yes' to these questions, you are probably **employed**

- Do you yourself have to do the work rather than hire someone else to do it for you?

- Can someone tell you at any time what to do or when to do it?

- Are you paid by the hour, week or month? Can you get overtime pay?

- Do you work set hours, or a given number of hours a week or month?

- Do you work at the premises of the person you work for or at a place or places he or she decides?

(For more information on this topic, see IR leaflet IR56)

Self-employed

If you can answer 'yes' to these questions, it will usually mean you are **self-employed**

- Do you have the final say in how the business is run?

- Do you risk your own money in the business?

- Are you responsible for meeting the losses as well as taking the profits?

- Do you provide the main items of equipment you need to do your job, not just the small tools many employees provide for themselves?

- Are you free to hire other people on your own terms to do the work you have taken on? Do you pay them out of your own pocket?

- Do you have to correct unsatisfactory work in your own time and at your own expense?

The tax situation for various occupations is examined below.

B. Authors, artists and entertainers

Authors, artists and entertainers, conducting a business on their own account and not employed at a salary, are assessed as income from trade. This means that they can charge against their income the expenses wholly and exclusively incurred in earning that income. The expenses would include: stationery, postage, materials used in the activity, the wardrobe of an actor, and the costs of a study or studio, such as heating, cleaning, rates and rent. If the work is done at home, a proportion of the actual outgoings associated with the accommodation may be charged. Income from royalties or from an outright sale of the work is assessable and must be included in the return, but a lump sum received on sale of the residual rights of a work can be spread forward up to six years, provided the work has been published for 10 years.

In the case of artists who have been engaged on a single work of art for over 12 months, the receipts obtained from such work can be spread for income tax purposes over the period during which it was made.

The 2001 Budget announced a change to this spreading arrangement. It has been replaced (for authors and creative artists) by an averaging of profits over two years. The first years available were 2000/01 and 2001/02.

From 1969, tax cannot be avoided by selling future earnings for a capital sum, this having become a fairly common practice in the theatrical profession.

From 1987/88, non-resident entertainers and sportsmen have had a withholding tax at the basic rate deducted from their UK earnings of at least £500.

Where a theatrical artist works under a contract of employment, his or her remuneration is chargeable to tax as income from employment, for which the deductible expenses are very limited. However, from 1990/91 the employed entertainer can deduct from his or her remuneration the fees paid to an agent who carries on an employment agency under licence. The fees deductible are limited to 17.5% of the emoluments. These provisions apply to a person who is employed as an actor, singer, musician, dancer or theatrical artist.

C. Divers

From 1978/79 the income of divers and diving supervisors operating in the UK or the continental shelf is chargeable as income from trade, and not as income from employment.

D. Farmers

(i) General. Subject to certain special arrangements noted below, farming is assessable to tax as income from trade. Assuming the farm is not operated as a limited company, losses incurred by individual farmers can be set off against other income, provided the farm is conducted with a view to profit. No set-off against other income is available to 'hobby farmers' (i.e. those operating without the expectation of profit) and not normally if losses have been incurred after 6 years. Hobby farmers can, however, claim for losses to be carried forward to be set off against any future profits. They may also claim relief against other income for the agricultural use of a farmhouse to the extent that this expenditure cannot be set off against farming income.

(ii) Averaging profits. After 1977/78 individual farmers and partnerships of farmers (not companies) have averaged profits over two consecutive years of assessment, where there is a difference of at least 30% in the profits of these years, with marginal relief for a difference between 25% and 30%.

(iii) Grants. Grants and other government subsidies are included in taxable profits if they represent revenue, not capital receipts.

(iv) Farmhouse. Only the expenses incurred in the business use of the farmhouse is allowed in computing farm profits for tax purposes.

(v) Herd basis. The 'herd' basis of assessment means that by an election within 2 years after the first year of assessment, production herds are treated as capital expenditure, not as stock in trade. Production herds are those intended for obtaining from them product for sale, such as wool and milk, but not livestock for resale in the normal course. Rearing costs and additions, but not replacements to the herd, are also capitalised and do not enter into the tax assessment, nor does the sale of the livestock. Sale of the products of the herd are, however, taxable.

(vi) VAT. Farmers are not required to register for VAT but may apply a fixed rate of 4% to sales of produce and this addition is recoverable by a VAT-registered customer.

(vii) Woodlands. The taxation of income from woodlands was abolished in 1988-89. However, for 1995/96 profit on short rotation coppice will be taxed as farming. This is where fast-growing trees are regularly harvested for fuel.

E. Ministers of religion

Ministers of religion may claim a deduction from income for expenses wholly, exclusively and necessarily incurred in carrying out their duties, e.g. motor and travelling expenses so incurred, postage, stationery, the replacement of robes, out-of-pocket payments to curates and lay workers, telephone charges, communion expenses, etc. A minister who pays the rent of his or her private residence may claim a deduction for whatever proportion of that residence is used in connection with his or her duties up to a maximum of one-quarter. A claim can also be made for lighting, heating, and so on, according to the proportion attributable to professional purposes. A case in 1986 decided that a vicar was not entitled to claim capital allowances for a slide projector, because he did not have to incur the expenditure for his work. However a vicar can claim capital allowance on his or her car and office furniture and equipment.

F. Cessation provisions

Certain self-employed professional persons, notably barristers, were until recently taxed on a 'cash basis' – that is, their tax computations cover only actual cash received and paid and do not include amounts due but unpaid. This practice meant that when they ceased to follow their profession, or retired, fees received in cash after cessation escaped tax.

The 1998 Finance Act revoked this privileged treatment of some professionals. It effectively means that those firms who had received authorisation to operate the 'cash basis' will have to include work-in-progress as defined by SSAP 9. Where time ledgers record staff time,then a useful starting point can be using the the proportion of the charge-out rate covering salaries and overhead recovery. Partners' work in progress would normally only include overhead allocation.

The main points of the legislation are as follows:

1. The accounts must be prepared to show a true and fair view of the profits.
2. The first year affected by these provisions is 1999/00.
3. The catch-up charge is payable over 10 years, starting with 1999/00, and there is a capping to restrict the additional charge to one tenth of the total amount or 10% of the normal profits of the business.
4. There is relief for any double charging when the firm first moved from an earnings basis for the first 7 years of practice.

The following points should also be noted:

a. Whilst the charge will be under Part 5 of ITTOA 2005 for the catch-up charge and therefore not liable to Class 4 NIC, losses could be offset against the charge and it will still count as net relevant earnings for pension purposes. It will not be possible to offset overlap relief against the catch-up charge. The taxpayer will be able to opt to pay the whole catch-up charge at once but unless told to the contrary the 10-year spreading provisions would apply. Also, it should be noted that where a sole practitioner ceases to practice, the 10-year spread will continue but this will be on a fixed one tenth of the charge basis.
b. Partnerships – where a new partner joins the firm, it will be spread between the partners for the year in which the deferred charge bites in the profit sharing ration of that year. It is important to note that incoming partners will be buying into the deferred catch-up charge.

G. Subcontractors in construction industry

Subcontractors in the construction industry are subject to a system which provides for deduction of tax at source on payments within the industry, unless the contractor holds an exemption certificate.

If a subcontractor holds a Gross Payment Certificate (GPC) issued by the Inland Revenue, the contractor may pay him gross. If he does not hold a GPC but does have a Registration Card, the contractor makes a tax deduction from the labour element of the payment (18%) which must then be paid over to the Inland Revenue.

If a subcontractor does not have either a GPC or a Registration Card, the contractor must treat him as an employee and payments to the subcontractor must be made under PAYE.

During 2003, the Inland Revenue gave notice that it intends to reform the Construction Industry Deduction Scheme. This has been deferred to 2006.

5

Capital Gains

Capital gains and capital losses refer to profits or losses on the sale or disposal otherwise of assets, including land and buildings, shares and securities, etc.; this does not include business stock held for sale, which is taxed through the normal process of taxing business profits. In essence a gain occurs when an asset is sold for more than it cost, and a loss is the reverse, but there are many qualifications to this simple statement, as will appear below. For sales after 5 April 1988 of assets held at 31 March 1982 the value at the latter date is normally substituted for the cost.

The tax applies to persons who are resident and ordinarily resident in the UK on gains arising both in the UK and abroad. The gains of husband and wife are assessed separately. Individuals do not pay tax on the first £8,500 in 2005/06 and £8,200 in 2004/05. There are many other exemptions (see below). Most trusts are exempt to half the usual rate. Full exemption will, however, apply to trusts for the mentally handicapped, persons receiving attendance allowance, and the middle or higher range of disability allowance.

5.2 RATES OF TAX

Limited companies

Both small and large companies bear corporation tax on their capital gains at the appropriate corporation tax rates.

Investment trusts, unit trusts and funds in court

The 1980 Finance Act gave these bodies complete exemption from capital gains. Investors are liable for capital gains tax on the realisation of their interests in the trusts.

Individuals

Individuals are liable to capital gains tax at their marginal rate of income tax. From 6 April 2000, gains are taxable at 10%, 20% or 40%.

Discretionary, accumulation and maintenance trusts, and personal representatives

With effect from 6 April 2004, the rate applicable to trusts is increased to 40% (previously 34%)

5.3 THE PRINCIPAL EXCEPTIONS

The following gains are not chargeable to the tax:

- The principal residence of an individual or a house which he or she owns and occupies or which is occupied rent free by a dependent relative before 6 April 1988, or where a person is required by the terms of his employment to live in other accommodation. See below for further comment.

- Vehicles of the private car type not used for business.

- Goods and chattels sold for no more than £6,000. For a sale price above these limits the gain is limited to 5/3rds of the excess.

- Certain forms of savings, such as: National Savings Certificates, National Development Bonds, Defence Bonds, Save As You Earn and TESSA bonuses, ISA gains and Premium Bonds.

- Sums received on the maturity or surrender of life assurance policies by the original owner, or where they are gifts to the taxpayer.

- Moveable property with predictable life of under 50 years, e.g. wasting assets, such as animals and boats, not subject to capital allowances. Special provisions apply to leases of 50 years or less. Other wasting assets must be written down progressively and only the balance of cost can be set against sale proceeds for capital gains purposes.

- The first £8,500 of capital gains in 2005/06 and £8,200 in 2004/05. Both husband and wife obtain this exemption.

- Gains on the disposal of British government securities and those guaranteed by the British government; and corporate bonds, debentures and loan stock, if the company has a quotation on a stock exchange, but not loans convertible into shares, unmarketable securities, those carrying excessive interest and those linked to a share index.

- Gifts to charities and the capital gains of charities.

- Gifts or sales by a taxpayer to his or her spouse, but in this case the spouse will be assumed to have acquired the asset at the date and cost when it was originally acquired.

- From 13 March 1989, gifts of certain business assets are available for hold over relief – see below under 'Gifts'.

- The first £4,250 of gains for trusts in 2005/06 (£4,100 in 2004/05), or £8,500 (£8,200 in 2004/05) for trusts for people with learning difficulties and those receiving the middle or higher rate of disability living allowance.

- The first holder of Business Expansion Scheme shares issued after 18 March 1986, and the first disposal of shares under the Enterprise Investment Scheme.

- Capital gains in personal equity plans.

- Capital gains which relate to the period before 1 April 1982.

- Transfers between husband and wife.

5.4 CALCULATING THE GAIN (INCLUDING INDEXATION)

The general method

A capital gain or loss is essentially the difference between the cost of an asset and the proceeds of sale, subject to 'rebasing' – see below. The costs include the incidental expenses incurred on acquisition or disposal, e.g. professional fees, commission and stamp duty. From the resultant gain an indexation allowance is deducted to offset inflation since 31 March 1982, or the date of acquisition, if later. The legislation is complex and special rules apply to part disposals of investments, disposals and acquisitions of investments in the same period of stock exchange account, investments pooled for tax purposes, transfers between company groups and disposals in company reorganisations and reconstructions.The March 1998 budget abolished the indexation allowance (not for companies) with effect from 6 April 1998. However, for an asset held before that date an allowance for indexation will be available up to 5 April 1998.

From 6 April 1998 onwards Tapering Relief is available (see below).

CGT simplification

The Finance Bill 2003 included measures to simplify the operation of CGT. For 2003/04 tax returns and subsequent years, individuals, trustees and personal representatives do not need to complete the Capital Gains pages of the tax return provided:

- the total of their chargeable gains, after taper relief, does not exceed their annual exempt amount, and
- the total proceeds from the sale of non-exempt assets in the year does not exceed four times the annual exempt amount for individuals (previously twice the annual amount).

This rule will not apply where taxpayers wish to utilise losses to offset against gains. In this case, the Capital Gains Tax pages will need to be completed.

Rebasing

Rebasing applies to assets held at 31 March 1982 and means that the value of the assets at that date is normally substituted for their cost in calculating a gain or loss. Subject to the following qualifications all disposals of these assets are rebased for disposals after 5 April 1988; previously the taxpayer had an option to do so.

It will be assumed that no loss or gain arises in the following circumstances:

● Where a gain arises on rebasing but a smaller gain or a loss would have arisen without rebasing, i.e. if the actual cost of an asset acquired before 31 March 1982 was set off against the sales proceeds.

● Where a loss arises on rebasing but either a smaller loss or a gain would have arisen without rebasing.

The foregoing assumptions will not apply if an election (irrevocable) is made for all assets (including those acquired before 6 April 1965) held at 31 March 1988 to be rebased, but only in special circumstances will such an election be beneficial. Unless rebased to 31 March 1982 the cost of assets held at 6 April 1965 was taken to be their value at that date, subject to a time apportionment for assets other than securities and development land, and subject to indexation from 31 March 1982. The value of assets at 6 April 1965 will, however, rarely be greater than their value at 31 March 1982.

Indexation

Gains after 31 March 1982 are reduced by applying to the cost the rise in the Retail Price Index since acquisition up to 5 April 1998, if the asset is disposed of after this date. The taxpayer may apply for indexation to be applied to the value of the asset rather than to the original cost. From 30 November 1993 indexation cannot be used to create or augment a loss. From 4 July 1987 indexation cannot be applied to shares in building societies or industrial and provident societies.

An example of indexation

The following example shows the calculation of the gain in a simple case where the asset was acquired in March 1987 and sold in October 1998. The indexation allowances for assets disposed of in April 1998 are shown below.

	£	£
Price received on sale	65,000	
Less: Incidental expenses on sale	2,000	
Net proceeds on sale		63,000
Price paid on acquisition	29,000	
Add: Incidental expenses on purchase	1,000	
Total cost of acquisition		30,000
Gain before indexation		33,000
Less: Indexation allowance		
£30,000 x 0.562 (162.6 – 104.1) / 104.1		16,860
NET GAIN		£16,140

Note that this particular gain is above the individual's exemption limit but would be added to other gains, less losses, for the tax year, and the exemption limit would be deducted from the total.

Capital Gains Tax Indexation Allowance

The gains arising on the disposal of an asset may be reduced by an indexation allowance which is calculated by reference to increases in the Retail Prices Index published by the Department of Employment. The allowance is available from March 1982 to April 1998

The Retail Price Index figures published are set out below.

For individuals, indexation is not available for assets acquired post 6 April 1998 and is replaced by taper relief (see Section 5.5 below).

There is no change for taxpayers liable to corporation tax, i.e. indexation still applies.

Prices at January 1987 = 100

Year	Jan	Feb	Mar	Apr	May	Jun	Jul	Aug	Sep	Oct	Nov	Dec
1982	-	-	79.44	81.04	81.26	81.85	81.88	81.90	81.85	82.26	82.66	82.51
1983	82.61	82.97	83.12	84.28	84.64	84.84	85.30	85.68	86.06	86.36	86.67	86.89
1984	86.84	87.20	87.48	88.64	88.97	89.20	89.10	89.94	90.11	90.67	90.95	90.87
1985	91.20	91.94	92.80	94.78	95.21	95.41	95.23	95.49	95.44	95.59	95.92	96.05
1986	96.25	96.60	96.73	97.67	97.85	97.79	97.52	97.82	98.30	98.45	99.29	99.62
1987	100.0	100.4	100.6	101.8	101.9	101.9	101.8	102.1	102.4	102.9	103.4	103.3
1988	103.3	103.7	104.1	105.8	106.2	106.6	106.7	107.9	108.4	109.5	110.0	110.3
1989	111.0	111.8	112.3	114.3	115.0	115.4	115.5	115.8	116.6	117.5	118.3	118.8

Year	Jan	Feb	Mar	Apr	May	Jun	Jul	Aug	Sep	Oct	Nov	Dec
1990	119.5	120.2	121.4	125.1	126.2	126.7	126.8	128.1	129.3	130.3	130.0	129.9
1991	130.2	130.9	131.4	133.1	133.5	134.1	133.8	134.1	134.6	135.1	135.6	135.7
1992	135.6	136.3	136.7	138.8	139.3	139.3	138.8	138.9	139.4	139.9	139.7	139.2
1993	137.9	138.8	139.3	140.6	141.1	141.0	140.7	141.3	141.9	141.8	141.6	141.9
1994	141.3	142.1	142.5	144.2	144.7	144.7	144.0	144.7	145.0	145.2	145.3	146.0
1995	146.0	146.9	147.5	149.0	149.6	149.8	149.1	149.9	150.6	149.8	149.8	150.7
1996	150.2	150.9	151.5	152.6	152.9	153.0	152.4	153.1	153.8	153.8	153.9	154.4
1997	154.4	155.0	155.4	156.3	156.9	157.5	157.5	158.5	159.3	159.5	159.6	160.0
1998	159.5	160.3	160.8	162.6	163.5	163.4	163.0	163.7	164.4	164.5	164.4	164.4
1999	163.4	163.7	164.1	165.2	165.6	165.6	165.1	165.5	166.2	166.5	166.7	167.3
2000	166.6	167.5	168.4	170.1	170.7	171.1	170.5	170.5	171.7	171.6	172.1	172.2
2001	171.1	172.0	172.2	173.1	172.2	174.4	173.3	174.0	174.6	174.3	173.6	173.4
2002	173.3	173.8	174.5	175.7	176.2	176.2	175.9	176.4	177.6	177.9	178.2	178.8
2003	178.4	179.3	179.9	181.2	181.5	181.3	181.3	181.6	182.5	182.6	182.7	183.5
2004	183.1	183.8	184.6	185.7	186.5	186.8	186.8	187.4	188.1	188.6	189.0	189.9
2005	188.9	189.6										

Using RI as the Retail Price Index for March 1982, if the asset was acquired prior to April 1981, or the month falling 12 months after the date on which the asset was acquired or expenditure incurred, and RD as the Retail Price Index for the month in which the disposal was made (or April 1998 if later and an individual), the indexation allowance is calculated by the formula:

$$\frac{RD - RI}{RI} \quad \text{rounded to the nearest third decimal place.}$$

5.5 TAPER RELIEF

Taper relief was introduced from 6 April 1998 in relation to the capital gains of individuals. It reduces the chargeable gain according to the length of time an asset has been held and whether the asset has been held as a business asset or a non-business asset.

Taper relief applies to net gains chargeable after the deduction of loss relief. For business assets, the minimum qualifying holding period before taper relief is available is one year. For non-business assets it is three years.

For non-business assets held on 17 March 1998, an additional year is added to the actual period of ownership.

Following announcements in the 2002 Budget, the rates of taper relief are:

	Number of whole years in qualifying holding period	Percentage of gain chargeable
Gains on disposals of business assets <u>post 6 April 2002</u>		
	1	50
	2	25
Gains on disposals of business assets <u>from 5 April 2000 to 5 April 2002</u>		
	1	87.5
	2	75
	3	50
	4	25
Gains on disposals of business assets <u>pre 6 April 2000</u>		
	1	92.5
	2	85
Gains on disposals of <u>non-business assets</u>		
	1	100
	2	100
	3	95
	4	90
	5	85
	6	80
	7	75
	8	70
	9	65
	10 or more	60

Thus it can be seen that there is a far more generous rate of relief for business assets. The definition as to what constitutes a business asset is therefore crucial. In broad terms, business assets include:

- assets used in an individual's own trade
- shares in an unlisted trading company
- shares in a listed trading company where the shareholder can exercise at least five percent of the voting rights
- shares owned by employees in the company for which they work provided they do not have a material interest of more than ten percent in the company
- shares owned by employees in the trading company where they work.

A new definition as to what constitutes a 'trading' company was introduced by the Finance Act 2002, based on the *activities* of a company and not, as previously, on its *purpose*.

From 6 April 2004, the definition of a business asset was extended in relation to periods of ownership after that date and disposals on or after that date.

In addition to everything that qualified as a business asset previously, assets used wholly or partly for the purposes of a trade carried on by an individual, the trustees of a settlement, the personal representatives of a deceased person, or certain partnerships, also qualify as business assets irrespective of whether the owner of the asset is actively involved in carrying out the trade.

If an asset is partly business and partly non-business, any gain on disposal of such an asset must be split into business and non-business parts on a just and reasonable basis. Taper relief is then applied to each part of the gain in the usual way.

5.6 TRUSTEES

Trustees are liable for capital gains on the sale of trust assets, at the income tax rate, but the beneficiaries under the trust will not be liable for the tax when they dispose of their interests under the trust. This provision has the effect of avoiding a double charge on the persons ultimately entitled to the benefit of the assets held in trust for them. (See also 5.1O Death of the Taxpayer.)

The beneficiary of an overseas trust is liable to pay capital gains tax on remittances to him or her of the trust's gains. There is no exemption from the tax when an interest in an overseas trust is disposed of. Measures to prevent tax avoidance by setting up overseas trusts were introduced in 1991/92.

5.7 LOSSES

Losses on the sale of assets can be set off against capital gains and any losses not used in this way can be carried forward. The loss concerned is the loss referable to the period after 31 March 1982 calculated in the manner indicated in section 5.4 above. For 1977/78 and onwards losses brought forward will be used only to the extent necessary to reduce gains to the exemption limit.

Losses incurred by individuals on the disposal of shares taken up in unquoted trading companies may be set off against income for income tax purposes; balances unrelieved in this way can be set off against capital gains.

Relief of capital gains tax applies to losses incurred from irrecoverable loans and payments under guarantees granted to borrowers for trading purposes. This relief is not applicable to loans between members of a group of companies.

5.8 SALE OF BUSINESS ON RETIREMENT

Retirement relief was available to individuals who made a 'qualifying disposal'. Essentially this meant:

1. a material disposal of business assets or
2. an associated disposal.

Business assets include the whole or part of a business and shares in a personal company which is either a trading company or the holding company of a trading group.

The relief was available to individuals aged 50 or more at the date of disposal. It was also given to individuals who were forced to retire before the age of 50 on grounds of ill health.

The relief has now been phased out, but in 2002/03, an individual's maximum amount of gains which could qualify for retirement relief were

a. £50,000 plus
b. 50% of the gain between £50,000 and £200,000.

From 2003/04 onward, retirement relief was abolished.

Retirement relief was given after indexation allowance but before taper relief.

5.9 REPLACEMENT OF ASSETS (ROLLOVER RELIEF)

This relief enables the payment of capital gains tax to be postponed, possibly indefinitely, when a business asset is sold and is replaced by another asset. It applies to land and buildings, fixed plant, ships and aircraft, property let commercially and let as furnished holiday accommodation, and goodwill, and it is not necessary that the new asset is of the same kind as the old asset. It does not apply to movable plant or machinery, farming, property development, or where half a company's assets are held in land, or motor cars.

In the case of the sale of a non-depreciating asset, e.g. land and buildings, the capital gain is set off against the cost of the new asset, deferring any capital gains tax payable until the new asset is sold. However, a gain on the sale of a new asset could again be rolled over by a further replacement and so on indefinitely. Rollover relief is available to landlords selling land or buildings to tenants who have rights to acquire the freehold reversions under the Leasehold Reform Act 1967 and the Housing and Urban Development Act 1993, provided reinvestment is made in replacement land and buildings.

Where a depreciating asset is sold the capital gain is not deducted from the cost of a replacement but is postponed for 10 years unless meanwhile the new asset has been sold or replaced by a non-depreciating asset. Depreciating assets are those with a predictable life of under 50 years such as boats and animals, and leases with an unexpired term of 60 years.

In all cases the new asset must be acquired not earlier than one year before and not later than three years after the sale of the old asset, but there can be some flexibility in these limits by agreement of the Inspector, in certain circumstances.

If the cost of a new asset is less than the gross proceeds from the sale of the old asset then the difference (if less than the gain) represents the capital gain on which tax must be paid and only the balance of the gain can be rolled over.

On and after 1 January 1993 rollover relief applies to EU quotas for the premium given to producers of ewes and calves and suckler cows, milk and potato quotas being already included since 1987.

From 20 June 1994 the amount of the gains which can be rolled over into a qualifying investment cannot exceed the acquisition cost of the replacement investment. The excess is not ever liable to tax.

Rollover relief applies when one company in a group transfers an asset to another group member at a gain. The relief does not apply to so-called 'roll around' when assets are transferred within a group but no replacement asset is acquired. The relief does apply where land is disposed of by one member of a group as a result of compulsory purchase, and replacement land is acquired by another group member. These provisions were announced in the 1994 Budget but have represented a long-standing practice.

5.10 DEATH OF THE TAXPAYER

No capital gains tax is payable but there may be a liability for inheritance tax (see Chapter 9). The persons who inherit the assets are assumed to take them at their market value at the date of death. This treatment applies to settled property on which the deceased had an interest.

Personal representatives can charge the expenses of establishing title in computing the gains or losses on the sale of assets in a deceased person's estate. Either the actual justifiable expenses can be charged or a scale effective after 5 April 1993 applied. From the same date corporate trustees must apply a further scale of charges for transfers of assets to beneficiaries and for actual disposals and acquisitions.

5.11 PAYMENT OF TAX

Payment is due on 31 January after the end of the tax year in which the gains accrued.

5.12 SALE OF PRIVATE HOUSE

As mentioned in section 5.3 above, capital gains tax is not payable on the sale of the principal private residence owned and occupied by a taxpayer. If the taxpayer owns and occupies more than one private residence he or she should advise the Inspector of Taxes which is to be treated as the principal private residence for exemption purposes. Subject to the qualifications set out below, the taxpayer will be liable for a proportion of the gain on the sale of the principal private residence corresponding to the periods when he or she was not in occupation of that house:

- Exemption applied to a house owned by the taxpayer and occupied rent free by a dependent relative before 6 April 1988.

- Absence due to having to live elsewhere under a contract of employment is ignored, e.g. a vicar who has to live in his or her parish; so is up to four years' total absences due to working away from home; and all absences while working abroad.

- Periods of absence of up to three years in total are ignored, and so are absences in the last three years for the purposes of selling the house.

- Full exemption applies where part of a house is let as residential accommodation, provided the part let does not exceed the part occupied by the taxpayer, with a maximum relief of £40,000.

- Where a taxpayer carries on a business in part of a house exclusively set aside for that purpose, there will be a liability for capital gains tax on that part. The mere use of non-exclusive facilities, even if a charge is claimed in the business assessment, should not, however, give rise to a capital gains assessment.

5.13 HUSBAND AND WIFE

With independent taxation of married women after 5 April 1990, the wife is liable for tax on the gains made from the disposal of the assets she owns. She will pay at her marginal rate of income tax, i.e. in 2004/05 and 2003/04, 10%, 20% and 40%, and will be entitled to her own annual exemption limit of £8,200 in 2004/05 (£7,900 in 2003/04). Where assets are owned jointly by husband and wife, any gain will be shared equally, in the absence of other evidence as to the ownership of shares. By transferring investments and other chargeable assets from one party to the other full advantage can be taken of each party's exemption limits. See 5.17 Bed and Breakfasting.

The Government has announced that civil partnerships formed as a result of the Civil Partnerships Act 2004 will be treated the same as married couples for tax purposes. Thus, from the start of the civil partnership scheme, tax charges and reliefs and anti-avoidance rules will apply equally to married couples and civil partners and those treated as such. The tax changes will take effect from 5 December 2005.

5.14 GIFTS

A gift from one person to another is a 'disposal' and if the market value of the asset at the time when the gift was made exceeds the cost, the difference is basically a capital gain. To the extent that an asset is transferred at a price below open market value the difference is treated as a gift. No tax is payable by the giver of a chattel when the gift is below the chattels exemption limit of £6,000. Nor would the giver be liable to capital gains tax where his total capital gains in a tax year were within the tax-free limits.

'Hold-over relief' for gifts made before 14 March 1989 had the effect of giving general relief to the giver but this general relief was cancelled on that date. Hold-over relief meant that the recipient of a gift took the asset for tax purposes at the market value less the capital gains made by the giver. The capital gains tax liability was thus deferred until the recipient sold or otherwise disposed of the gifted asset. This relief now applies only to gifts of certain business and other assets to a UK resident. The assets concerned are as follows: assets of a trade, profession, vocation or family company including shares in a family trading company or in unquoted trading companies; agricultural property where the giver has vacant possession; heritage property; charitable gifts and those to political parties (with some qualifications) and housing associations; and capital paid from accumulation and maintenance trusts not later than payments of income.

After 13 March 1989 capital gains tax may be paid by ten equal annual instalments on disposals of land, unquoted shares, and controlling holdings of quoted shares, subject to an election being made. The Inland Revenue Shares Valuation Office will value unquoted shares at 31 March 1982 where all shareholders with similar holdings agree.

5.15 COMPANY LEAVING GROUP

Where a company leaves a group any asset acquired from another group member within the preceding 6 years is a deemed disposal of the asset at the date of acquisition. The chargeable gain or loss accrues immediately before the company left the group. The 1994 Budget contained measures to prevent tax avoidance by artificial degrouping.

5.16 REINVESTMENT IN EIS SHARES

Investors may defer gains made on any assets by investing in shares which, broadly, qualify for relief under the Enterprise Investment Scheme (EIS). Re-investment in EIS shares must be made within the period one year before to three years after the gain accrues.

The shares must be newly issued and fully paid. Relief is not available for shares purchased from another investor.

The amount of the gain that can be deferred is the lower of:

1.   the amount subscribed by the investor for EIS shares, or
2.   the amount specified in the claim.

Note that there is no limit of £200,000 (£150,000 pre-6 April 2004) per annum to the amount of gains that can be deferred under this provision. The £200,000 limit relates to the EIS income tax relief provisions.

The deferred gain will become chargeable if:

a. the investor disposes of the new shares, or
b. the shares cease to be eligible for relief within 3 years of issue, or
c. the investor becomes non-resident and not ordinarily resident within 3 years of the shares being issued.

Taper relief is available for the period of ownership of the original asset, but not for the period of ownership of the new EIS shares.

5.17 BED AND BREAKFASTING

'Bed and Breakfasting' is a stock market expression describing the practice of selling shares, then immediately repurchasing them in order to crystalise capital gains (to utilise an annual exemption) or losses (to offset other gains). Typically a sale late on day 1 is followed by a similar purchase early on day 2, when hopefully the price will be much the same.

However, following the 1998 budget, disposals and acquisitions by individuals or trustees of shares of the same class in the same company within a 30-day period are to be matched for capital gain so that no gain or loss is realised.

However, there is currently no prohibition on shares being sold by one spouse on day 1 and 'repurchased' by the other spouse on day 2.

6

Rents from Property

6.1 GENERAL

In general rent and other income, less allowable expenses, receivable from the letting of land and buildings is assessable to tax. This applies whether the letting is furnished or unfurnished, of a single room, or of a major block of buildings or area of land. The exception is the situation of mutual trading, as where rents are received from its members by a housing association not conducted for profit.

On and after 6 April 1995 all income from property in the UK, whether from furnished or unfurnished letting, is pooled and assessed as income from property. The computation will generally follow the rules applicable to trading profits, using standard accounting principles, but the income is regarded as investment income. Capital allowances continue to apply where applicable, including wear and tear allowances for furnished letting. Losses can be set off against pooled income and unrelieved losses can be carried forward. Income from overseas property will generally follow the above rules but will be assessable separately. Corporation tax on let property is unaffected.

6.2 UNFURNISHED AND FURNISHED LETTINGS

Rents received less certain expenses are taxable on a 'current year' basis. Payment of the tax is as for Self-Assessment: two payments on account and a balancing payment – the first is paid on 31 January in the tax year, the second on 31st July following the tax year, and the final balancing payment made the next 31 January. The payments on account are 50% (each) of the previous year's liability. Application may be made to reduce these payments if rents are falling, but interest payments may be made if the amount reduced is excessive. The net rents which are chargeable to tax may be those due under a weekly tenancy or even under a lease granted for hundreds of years.

The expenses which may be deducted for tax purposes from the rental income cover: maintenance and repair of the property, services provided, insurance, rates, rent payable, capital allowances or 10% wear and tear allowance on equipment provided and management expenses such as agent's commission for obtaining tenants and for rent collection. These expenses must have been incurred during the currency of the lease, so that expenses incurred before the landlord under assessment took over the premises cannot be charged. Capital expenditure, such as the cost of extensions and improvements to premises, is disallowed. See chapter 4 – Business Taxation – for details of new 100% relief for making available flats above commercial premises.

Capital allowances cannot be claimed on plant and machinery in a let dwelling house, but capital allowances may be claimed on plant and machinery used for the maintenance and management of the property. If the landlord occupies part of the premises let, the expenses must be apportioned on an equitable basis.

The following is an example of a lettings computation.

	£	£
Rents receivable		20,000
Less: expenses:		
Water rates	3,000	
Maintenance of property	500	
Maintenance of furniture, etc.	250	
Insurance of furnishings	500	
Cleaning and other services.	600	
Wear and tear allowance – normally at		
10% of rent less water rates		
= 10% (20,000 – 3,000)	1,700	
		6,550
Taxable profit		13,450

Note: If only part of a house was let, the total council tax, water rates and other expenses would need apportioning on a reasonable basis, e.g. on floor space.

Where gross rents do not exceed £15,000, it is only necessary to submit to the Inspector of Taxes a statement showing gross income, total expenses and profit.

Losses may be carried forward to be set off against future profits, remembering that from 6 April 1995 all income from property is pooled.

Apportionments of premiums received for leases granted for 50 years or less are treated as rent in the year when the lease was granted. The basis of the calculation is the premium less one fiftieth for each year of the lease after the first year. For example, if a lease is granted for ten years at a premium of £2,000, the following amount is to be added to the rent in the first year:

Premium	£2,000
Less $\dfrac{10-1}{50} \times £2,000$	360
	£1,640

A premium will be assumed where the tenant agrees to carry out work, or to make a payment in lieu of rent or as consideration for the surrender of the lease.

Business rents and connected persons. 'Connected persons' mean generally close relatives of individuals, and companies under common control. Where rent, such as for business premises, is paid between connected persons, it will, after 10 March 1992, be assessed on the recipient as it accrues, not when it is actually received. This applies to rent payable in arrears and when it is an allowable expense for business purposes. The object of the rule is to prevent deferment of tax by the recipient of the accruing income.

Short lets. It is not always appreciated that returns must be made to the Inspector of Taxes of profits from the occasional letting of rooms and that these profits are liable to tax. The consequence of a failure to make returns may be an estimated assessment going back many years, interest and possible penalties. (But see 6.4 below, Rent a Room Scheme.)

6.3 FURNISHED HOLIDAY LETTINGS

The letting of furnished holiday accommodation is basically taxed in the same way as other furnished lettings. However, letting of holiday accommodation 'on a commercial basis' can be treated as a trade, with consequent tax advantages.

For the letting to be treated as a trade the holiday accommodation must be available to the public generally for at least 140 days in a year, must in fact be let for a total of 70 days, and must not be in the same occupation for a continuous period of more than 31 days. These periods can be averaged where a number of lettings in different premises are made.

As for other furnished lettings, the assessment is on the current year's profits and tax is payable in two instalments on 31 January in the year of assessment and the following 31 July. A loss can be carried forward or carried back for three years. Capital allowances may be claimed. Note that the rents may be subject to VAT if they exceed £60,000 from 1April 2005 (previously £58,000).

Hold-over relief for capital gains is available on disposal of the property.

The letting of caravans on a commercial basis is also normally assessable as trading income.

6.4 RENT A ROOM SCHEME

A relief was introduced from 1992/93 for individuals – owner occupiers and tenants – who let furnished accommodation in their only or main home.

Gross annual rents from this letting which do not exceed £4,250 in 2005/06 will be exempt from income tax altogether. Where the income exceeds £4,250, the person receiving the rent can either:

- pay tax on the amount by which the gross rent exceeds £4,250, without any further tax deduction for expenses, or

- pay tax on the profit (gross rents less actual expenses) in the normal way.

Where the rent is received jointly, such as in the case of a married couple sharing the income or by other than the resident, the limit of £4,250 is reduced by half to £2,125.

See Inland Revenue leaflet 'Rooms to let' (IR 87).

7

Miscellaneous Matters

7.1 ADDITIONAL ASSESSMENTS

Where the Inspector of Taxes discovers that there has been an undercharge to tax, the Revenue has the authority to make an additional assessment at any time up to five years from the filing date of the return.

If, however, there has been fraud or negligent conduct on the part of the taxpayer or a person acting on his or her behalf, the five-year limit is inoperative and additional assessments can be made for more than five years. A uniform time limit of 20 years applies for the recovery of tax in the case of default. But whatever reason why income was not brought into charge earlier, assessments of this kind relating to income arising before the date of death cannot be made on the executors or administrators of a deceased person after the end of the third year following the year of assessment in which the person died.

Where the taxpayer has acted fraudulently, the Revenue authorities are permitted to impose penalties of varying sums as well as such additional assessments as may be appropriate. Failure to notify liability to tax can involve a penalty up to the amount of tax unpaid. In some instances the mitigation of penalties is allowed and, where that is so, the individual is invariably dealt with more leniently when he has voluntarily made a full and complete disclosure of the facts before their discovery by the Inspector. Penalty negotiations, particularly where large sums are involved, need to be handled with extreme care, and the assistance of an adviser well experienced in these negotiations is recommended.

7.2 CLUBS AND SOCIETIES

Many clubs, societies and other unincorporated associations are formed for the mutual benefit of the members and to provide communal services. These associations are generally considered to be 'companies' for taxation purposes and are therefore basically liable to corporation tax on trading, investment and letting income, as well as capital gains. Approved charitable associations are exempt, however, from tax. Many supplies used by charities are zero-rated for VAT.

The subscriptions and contributions payable by members are not normally taxable, nor are payments made by club members for goods and facilities which the club is set up to provide for them. On the basis that members' subscriptions and other receipts are applied to meet the running expenses of the club, they are not chargeable for the purpose of calculating the profit assessable for corporation tax. Corporation tax will, however, be payable on the following:

- Activities which constitute trading, such as the holding of sales, sporting events, displays and the letting of club facilities for private purposes, and in these cases the applicable expenses can be set off against the income. However, tax will not normally be charged where the club makes it known that the profits from a particular event will be donated to charity and there is no regular trading or competition with other traders.

- Interest received, such as from bank deposits or from government or local authority stock, and including interest on national savings, but not dividends from UK companies. Where income tax is deducted from the interest, it can be set off against any corporation tax payable by the club, but the interest gross of income tax is chargeable in the corporation tax assessment. Building society interest must be grossed up for income tax by adding ¼ to the amount received and the income tax is likewise deductible from the gross corporation tax. Note that dividends received from UK companies are not chargeable to corporation tax and the tax credit on the dividend cannot be reclaimed.

For the financial year starting 1 April 2005, clubs and societies with profits chargeable to Corporation Tax of less than £10,000 will pay no Corporation Tax. For profits between £10,000 and £50,000, Corporation Tax will be charged at 23.75%. Profits greater than £50,000 but less than £300,000 will be charged to Corporation Tax at 19%.

In any event, provided they do not carry out competitive trading but apply surpluses to charities or club purposes, they should be able to avoid paying corporation tax, except on interest receivable.

7.3 THE COUNCIL TAX

The nature of the tax

In England, Scotland and Wales, the former Community Charge was replaced by the Council Tax from 1 April 1993. Domestic rates are still payable in Northern Ireland. Half the council tax consists of a personal element based on the residents in a dwelling, subject to the number of exceptions and reliefs; the other half is a property element based on the value of the property, also subject to exemptions. Dwellings were valued at their saleable value on 1 April 1991 but there is provision for appeals against the valuations if made before the beginning of the council tax year.

In England, the valuations were placed in bands as follows:

Band	Values
A	up to £40,000
B	£ 40,001 to 52,000
C	£ 52,001 to 68,000
D	£ 68,001 to 88,000
E	£ 88,001 to 120,000
F	£120,001 to 160,000
G	£160,001 to 320,000
H	above £320,000

Different bands exist for properties in Scotland and Wales.

Exempt dwellings

Dwellings exempt from tax are those exclusively occupied by students and certain empty properties. Exempt properties are: those which have been empty and unfurnished for 6 months; those left empty by someone entering hospital, a nursing home or residential care home; those left empty as a result of the death of the occupier and pending probate or letters of administration; those left empty for 6 months due to structural alterations. The owner is liable for the tax if the property is empty but not exempt, or if it is not the sole or main residence of the owner, such as a holiday home.

The persons liable

The tax is payable by the resident of a dwelling and that person may be the owner, leaseholder or licensee of the premises. Joint owners are jointly responsible for the tax. If there are no residents of properties not exempt, only the property element (50%) is payable. With one resident the tax is reduced by 25%.

Traders and landlords are relieved from the proportion of the charge applicable to the trade or the letting.

Reliefs

The following people living in a dwelling do not count as residents for the purpose of the tax: persons under 18; students; apprentices and VTS trainees; the severely impaired mentally. Residents who are disabled persons requiring extra space or rooms (such as downstairs bathrooms) are entitled to have the valuation of the premises placed in the next lower band, but there is no band lower than A. 80% of the tax is normally payable by persons receiving income support.

Payment by employer

Tax paid by an employer for an employee will be treated as a taxable benefit of the employee.

7.4 ERROR OR MISTAKE

It may happen that in completing his or her income tax return, the taxpayer makes a mistake which results in an excessive assessment. For example, an employed person may omit to claim the deduction of expenses wholly, exclusively and necessarily incurred in the performance of his duties; non-taxable capital receipts may have been included in business profits. Relief may be claimed for tax paid in respect of excessive assessments arising through an error or mistake, and claims may be made within five years from the filing date of the return. Relief is not given where the excessive assessment was made according to the practice then generally prevailing.

A taxpayer, finding that he has inadvertently made a mistake in a return or other statement resulting in the under-payment of tax, should immediately disclose the fullest details to his Inspector of Taxes, since failure to do so may well make it difficult to refute a more serious charge in the event of the Revenue authorities discovering the matter for themselves.

However, from the introduction of self-assessment in 1997, the submission of an incorrect, incomplete or late return will lead to the imposition of an automatic penalty. The penalty is £100 plus interest on tax paid late and on the penalty itself! Another penalty is levied every 6 months.

7.5 INCOME FROM ABROAD

The tax rules generally

The essential tax rules, which have many qualifications, but largely depend on residential status or domicile (see below), are as follows:

- UK residents are liable for UK tax on income and capital gains whether arising in the UK or elsewhere.

- Non-residents are liable for UK tax on income arising in the UK but not on income arising outside the UK.

- Domicile affects inheritance tax and capital gains. For individuals domiciled in the UK, inheritance tax is payable on assets wherever arising. Those not domiciled in the UK may incur liability to inheritance tax on UK assets.

The rules tend to be complex and, except in simple situations, merit expert advice.

Residence and domicile

Ordinary residence generally means living in the UK year after year on a permanent basis; but an individual who goes abroad permanently may still be regarded as ordinarily resident in the UK if visits to the UK are made 183 days or more in a tax year, or for an average of 91 days or more in each tax year calculated on a maximum of 4 years. Ordinary residence (but not 'residence') may be retained by going abroad for a holiday lasting more than a tax year, and certainly for visits abroad for less than a year.

An individual is strictly a 'resident' in the UK if he or she lives in the country for any period, but there are a number of exemptions for short visits – see Section 7.8. In particular the status of being resident applies (a) for a stay of 183 days or more in a tax year; (b) on coming to the UK permanently; (c) on coming to the UK for at least 3 years; and (d) a stay in the UK for employment for at least 2 years.

A taxpayer's domicile is his or her natural and permanent home. It affects liability to inheritance tax and capital gains tax. A domicile of origin applies to an individual at birth and is that of the father, or the mother of an illegitimate child or one whose father has died. This may be changed to a domicile of choice on attaining 16 years of age. Certain dependent people may be incapable of choosing a domicile and will assume a domicile of dependency.

Crown employees are liable to UK tax wherever they may reside.

The Government is currently reviewing the residence and domicile rules as they affect the taxation of individuals, and has (in April 2003) published a background paper for consultation.

Personal allowances

The general rule is that only individuals resident in the UK or Ireland are entitled to UK personal allowances. This rule is qualified by the fact that the following non-residents obtain full allowances:

- All citizens from European Economic Area (from 6 April 1996);
- Commonwealth citizens;
- Crown employees, including civil servants and members of the armed forces, and their widows or widowers;
- Employees of UK missionary societies:
- Residents in the Isle of Man or Channel Islands;
- Former residents in the UK who live abroad for health reasons and relatives who live with them;
- Where a double taxation agreement allows a claim to the allowance.

Temporary residence abroad

A person who leaves the UK for a stay abroad of less than a full tax year (6 April to the following 5 April) normally remains a UK resident for tax purposes. If, however, a person goes abroad for a complete tax year or longer to carry on a trade or profession, the UK residential status is lost from the date of leaving the UK although UK tax allowances continue to apply for the tax year of leaving. Where the person goes abroad for any other reason, UK residential status is retained until the habit of life indicates otherwise. The retention of a place of abode in the UK, a stay in the UK for 183 days or more in a tax year and visits to the UK for 91 days or more in any year, averaged over 5 years, are evidence that UK residential status has been retained.

Permanent residence abroad

Where an individual leaves the UK for permanent residence abroad, the liability for UK tax is computed by reference to the period of residence in the UK. In other words, the tax year is split by the date of departure (and, if applicable, return). If such an individual returns to the UK before the end of the tax year following the tax year of departure the concession will not apply. The concession is extended to years of departure and return when an individual leaves the UK for full-time employment abroad for at least a complete tax year. Interim visits to the UK are limited to 183 days in a tax year or an average of 91 days over up to 4 years. Taxation of an accompanying spouse is also covered by this concession.

Non-residents – double taxation agreements

A person who is considered resident abroad is, in principle, liable to UK tax on income from the UK, but not on income from overseas sources. Such a person is also likely to be liable to the tax levied by the country of residence on his or her total income. Where, however, a double taxation agreement exists between the UK and the overseas country, double taxation is avoided by means of the following calculation:

(1) Calculate the tax which would be payable on the UK income alone, after deducting applicable UK allowances from that income.

(2) Calculate the UK tax which would be payable on the total income, UK as well as overseas income, after deducting UK allowances from that total income. Multiply the UK tax so calculated by the fraction:

$$\frac{\text{UK income}}{\text{Total income}}$$

(3) The UK tax payable is the greater of the amounts arrived at in (1) and (2) above and, unless the UK income is very large, will normally be the result of the second calculation.

Non-residents – tax-free interest

A further relief to non-residents is that they can arrange for interest on certain UK government stocks to be paid to them without deduction of UK tax; or if the tax has been deducted to claim repayment from the Inspector of Foreign Dividends. The stock in question includes: Exchequer Bonds, Funding Loan, Savings Bonds, Victory Bonds and 3½% War Stock.

Employment abroad with an overseas employer

Tax relief on foreign earnings was abolished by the 1998 budget, with effect from 17 March 1998. Prior to that, if a British resident was employed abroad by an overseas employer for 365 days or more, the whole of the overseas earnings was free of UK tax, but a return had to be made to the UK authorities. In calculating the period abroad the taxpayer was allowed to count one-sixth of the period as continuous if he or she were on leave in the UK. In other words, if he or she spent more than one-sixth of the period on visits to the UK deduction from earnings would not be available. For a stay of 365 days or more abroad the period allowed in the UK was 62 days. The taxpayer is not assessed on certain expenses paid by the overseas employer, such as travel to and from the foreign country and hotel expenses. The remuneration from the overseas employer must be strictly applicable to the overseas employment.

Where, owing to the Gulf war, employees in Iraq or Kuwait had to return to the UK earlier than expected, they did not lose their exemption for foreign earnings.

Returning from overseas

The exemption from UK tax on foreign earnings basically applies to those who have retained their ordinary residence in the UK – that is, where the period abroad is short. Up to 5 April 1992 it was the practice of the Inland Revenue to give the exemption also to those who became ordinarily resident abroad as a result of a longer stay. But this practice ceased for those returning to the UK after 5 April 1992 so that terminal leave pay received in the UK after that date will be subject to UK tax. It may be possible to avoid this liability by arranging for the leave pay to be received while resident abroad or to have the leave period treated as residence abroad.

Overseas business or employment

Where a person is entitled to income from a trade, profession or vocation carried on abroad he or she will be assessable to UK tax on the whole of the income arising from that business. The assessment will be in the normal course on a preceding year basis (as applicable to an unincorporated business) and the taxpayer has the option of substituting the actual income of the period. It will be observed that an assessment on a business would be preferable to one as an employee, because of the allowance of business expenses in the former case.

However, if the employee bears the cost of travel to and from his employment abroad, or the cost of board and lodgings abroad, that cost can be deducted from his salary. Similarly the cost of two journeys to and from abroad by a spouse or child under 18 to visit the taxpayer is deductible where the employee spends 60 days or more continuously abroad; so is the cost of two journeys by the taxpayer to the UK to see a spouse or child. In 1986/87 and onwards, if the employer pays the cost of travel, an unlimited number of journeys are tax free in the hands of the employee.

The Inland Revenue can in 1993/94 and onwards require the payer of an employee to collect tax under PAYE where the employee works for a person other than his or her employer. This applies where the employer is based either overseas or in the UK (T.A. 1988 S.203B).

In some cases the precise amount of taxable remuneration is not known at the time of payment to employees who work both in the UK and abroad. The taxable remuneration may have to be estimated when paid and subject to PAYE. This applies only to remuneration for UK duties for non-resident employees and also on remittances to the UK of payments for overseas duties in the case of employees who are not ordinarily resident in the UK.

Absence on business abroad

The foregoing provisions also until 1984/85 covered the case of an individual (including a partner) who was absent from the UK on business for at least 30 qualifying days. The relief applied to an individual who was resident in the UK and carried on a trade, profession or vocation chargeable to tax on trade. The absence abroad must have been exclusively for the purpose of the business. The proportion of the income assessable is the proportion which the qualifying days abroad bear to 365 days. In the case of a partnership the income to be apportioned was the partner's share of the assessable partnership income after capital allowances but before loss relief.

Pensions from overseas sources

Where a UK resident receives a pension from overseas sources, and the British government has assumed responsibility for the payment, the whole amount of the pension is assessable in 1974/75 onwards, and not, as previously, merely the amount remitted to the UK. However, a deduction of 1/10th of the pension is allowed, or the whole of it for a pension payable for victims of National Socialist (Nazi) persecution in Germany or Austria.

7.6 INTEREST ON TAX

Interest on repayments

Interest, called a 'repayment supplement', is payable by the Inland Revenue in the case of a repayment of income tax or capital gains tax. If the repayment results from excess interim payments on account, interest will run from the actual dates the excess payments were received (i.e. usually around 31 January in the tax year and the following 31 July). To the extent the repayment results from an error in the balancing payment made on the 31 January following the tax year concerned, interest will run from this date as well.

Interest is also due on a repayment to a company of corporation tax, tax credits or investment income, or tax suffered by deduction. In this case the repayment is made after the end of 12 months from the latest date when the corporation tax was payable on the company's profits. The individual company must be resident in the UK. The interest is not taxable.

Interest on tax overdue

Subject to some special exceptions, interest is chargeable on tax unpaid. Historically interest below £30 was not charged but the use of computers now allows the increased ability to charge for all late payments of tax. The interest is not an allowable expense for tax purposes.

7.7 DISCRETIONARY AND ACCUMULATION TRUSTS

With effect from 6 April 2004, the rate applicable to trusts is increased to 40% (previously 34%). This change applies to:

- the income of discretionary and accumulation trusts other than dividends
- the capital gains of all trusts and estates of deceased persons in administration, and
- certain amounts received by all trusts (e.g. gains from offshore funds).

The separate trust rate of tax of 25% relating to dividends and similar income received by trusts is increased to 32.5%.

When a beneficiary receives a payment of income from the trust he or she obtains a tax credit of the overall rate applying at the time of payment. From 6 April 1995 bank interest payable to these trusts from UK banks was subject to deduction of tax at the basic rate of 25% – from 6 April 1996 at the lower rate of 20%. But the trustee must account for the extra 14% (34% – 20%).

From 6 April 1995 the rules applicable to the taxation of trust income have been simplified and are essentially as follows:

- If the settlor or the settlor's spouse has retained an interest in the trust, the income is treated as that of the settlor for tax purposes.

- The income is also treated as that of the settlor where the trust or settlement is in favour of the settlor's minor unmarried child.

- Where the settlor or the settlor's spouse receives a loan from the trustees, or makes a loan to them, the settlor is liable to income tax on the annual value of the loan, by reference to a statutory rate of interest.

7.8 VISITORS TO THE UK

Individuals covered

This section gives a general guide to the position of foreign-domiciled nationals who stay in the UK for substantial periods and receive income here. It also applies to British nationals when they return to the UK after long periods abroad, having meanwhile lost their UK residential status. The subject tends to be specialised and in a complicated situation expert advice is desirable.

Residence

The crucial question is whether the visitor is considered to have become resident in the UK. The general rules covering residence in the UK are as follows:

- An individual is not to be considered resident in the UK if here for a temporary purpose only, but will be regarded as resident if he or she spends more than 183 days here in any tax year to 5 April.

- Residence in the UK will be assumed if the individual visits the UK year after year for three years, spending three months here each year.

- Before 6 April 1993 residence in the UK was assumed where a visitor has a place of abode here, unless he or she works full time outside the UK, and in the later case duties performed in the UK are only incidental to the overseas employment. On and after 6 April 1993 the existence of available accommodation is ignored in determining residential status.

- Where a visitor acquires a lease of three years or more for accommodation in the UK he or she will become ordinarily resident from the following dates:
  (i) From the date of arrival if the lease is acquired in the tax year of arrival;
  (ii) From the beginning of the tax year of acquiring the lease if acquired after the tax year of arrival.

Where there is no intention of remaining in the UK for three years, and no three-year lease of accommodation is acquired, the visitor does not become ordinarily resident until the beginning of the tax year after the third anniversary of arrival.

UK tax liability

- Non-residents. No UK tax is payable on income, e.g. pay, arising overseas. Income arising in the UK is, however, liable for UK tax at the basic rate and no personal allowances can be obtained.

- Residents. Individuals becoming resident here are liable for UK tax and are entitled to full personal allowances for the tax year in which they arrive.

Liability to UK tax is computed by reference to the period of residence in the following situations:

- Where an individual takes up permanent residence in the UK or intends to stay in the UK for at least three years.

- Where an individual takes up employment in the UK expected to last for at least two years.

- An individual who becomes resident in the UK is liable to capital gains tax on gains accruing after arrival in the UK and before departure.

7.9 STAMP DUTY

Some kinds of transfers are subject to Stamp Duty, such as the transfers of shares, transfers of property and certain instruments such as declarations of trust. From 30 November 2001, stamp duty exemption is available for the purchase of property in certain designated disadvantaged areas of the UK, and where the consideration or premium for a lease does not exceed £150,000.

Stamp taxes from Budget day (7April) to 30 November 2003

Transfer of property (consideration paid)

		Disadvantaged areas	
Rate	All property	Residential	Non-residential
0%	£0-£60,000	£0-£150,000	All
1%	Over £60,000-£250,000	Over £150,000-£250,000	
3%	Over £250,000-£500,000	Over £250,000-£500,000	
4%	Over £500,000	Over £500,000	

New leases (lease duty), **Duty on rent**

Term	Rate of charge on average annual rent
Not exceeding 7 years	* 1%
More than 7 years but not exceeding 35 years	2%
More than 35 years but not exceeding 100 years	12%
More than 100 years	24%

* applies only where the rent exceeds £5,000 per annum

Duty on **premium** is the same as for transfers of property (Except special rules apply for premiums where rent exceeds £600 annually)

Stamp taxes from 1 December 2003 (implementation of stamp duty land tax)

Transfers of property (consideration paid)

Rate	Land in disadvantaged areas Residential	Non-residential	All other land in the UK Residential	Non-residential
0%	£0-£150,000	All	£0-£60,000	£0-£150,000
1%	Over £150,000 -£250,000		Over £60,000 -£250,000	Over £150,000 -£250,000
3%	Over £250,000 -£500,000		Over £250,000 -£500,000	Over £250,000 -£500,000
4%	Over £500,000		Over £500,000	Over £500,000

Property that is not land, shares or interests in partnerships will no longer be subject to stamp duty

New leases – proposed duty on rent (subject to consultation)

Rate	Net present value of rent Residential	Non-residential
0%	£0-£60,000	£0-£150,000
1%	Over £60,000	Over £150,000

Duty on **premium** is the same as for transfers of property (Except special rules apply for premiums where rent exceeds £600 annually)

The rate of **stamp duty** and **stamp duty reserve tax** on the **transfer of shares and securities** is unchanged at 0.5% for 2004/05, rounded up to the nearest £5.

Stamp Duty Land Tax Rates from 17 March 2005

Transfers of land and buildings (consideration paid)

Rate	Land in disadvantaged areas		All other land in the UK	
	Residential	**Non-residential**	**Residential**	**Non-residential**
0%	£0-£150,000	£0-£150,000	£0-£120,000	£0-£150,000l
1%	Over £150,000 -£250,000	Over £150,000 -£250,000	Over £120,000 -£250,000	Over £150,000 -£250,000
3%	Over £250,000 -£500,000	Over £250,000 -£500,000	Over £250,000 -£500,000	Over £250,000 -£500,000
4%	Over £500,000	Over £500,000	Over £500,000	Over £500,000

NB - **Disadvantaged Area Relief** for non-residential land transactions **is not available for non-residential land transactions with an effective date on or after 17 March 2005.**

However, the relief is preserved for:

• the completion of contracts entered into and subsequently performed on or before 16 March 2005

• the completion or substantial performance of other contracts entered into on or before 16 March 2005, provided that there is no variation or assignment of the contract or sub-sale of the property after 16 March 2005 and that the transaction is not in consequence of the exercise after 16 March 2005 of an option or right of pre-emption.

New leases (lease duty) - duty on rent

Rate	Net present value of rent	
	Residential	**Non-residential**
0%	£0-£120,000	£0-£150,000
1%	Over £120,000	Over £150,000

NB - When calculating duty payable on the 'NPV' (Net Present Value) of leases, you must reduce your 'NPV' calculation by the following **before** applying the 1% rate.

Residential - £120,000   Non-residential - £150,000

Duty on **premium** is the same as for transfers of land (except special rules apply for premium where rent exceeds £600 annually).

The rate of **stamp duty/ stamp duty reserve tax** on the **transfer of shares and securities** is unchanged at 0.5% for 2005/06.

8

Value Added Tax

VAT came into effect for transactions made on and after 1 April 1973 and replaced purchase tax and the selective employment tax. The legislation is contained in the Value Added Tax Act 1994, as amended by the subsequent Finance Acts, and detailed provisions set out in numerous statutory orders issued from time to time.

The rate for most taxable goods and services not zero-rated became 17½% from 1 April 1991. Increasingly, a 5% band is being expanded, including fuel and power for domestic or charity use, installation of energy-saving materials, children's car seats and certain residential conversions.

VAT is a common method of indirect taxation in the European Union and, subject to variations of treatment amongst the member States, is made obligatory by a Directive of the Council of the EU. In the UK it takes the form of a charge on the invoiced value of applicable goods and services made by traders who are not exempt. The amount so charged to customers may be set against the VAT suffered by the trader on his or her purchases; in some cases this calculation may lead to a repayment of tax to the trader. The tax suffered by a business on its purchases is called 'input tax' and that which it charges its customers is called the 'output tax'.

The system operates right through the chain of importation or production of goods, through the distribution via wholesalers, until the final sale from the retailer to the consumer. It is thus the ultimate consumer who bears the tax on the sale price of purchases. As will be seen from the example below, the tax eventually takes the form of a tax on value added to basic raw materials or services.

Some goods and services are 'exempt' from the tax, and this means that the trader will not be able to charge the tax on sales to customers nor be able to obtain a credit for 'input tax' on relevant purchases. Exemption from all goods sold also applies to traders with a turnover of no more than £60,000 from 1 April 2005 (£58,000 previously) but exemption may not be an advantage since, although they cannot charge their customers with the tax, they are unable to claim credit for input tax suffered.

Many categories of goods and services are 'zero-rated'. This also means that the trader dealing in such goods cannot charge customers with the tax but can claim credit for relevant input tax.

8.2 THE SYSTEM ILLUSTRATED

Assuming that the goods are taxable and not zero-rated, and that the traders concerned are not exempt but are 'registered' with the Customs and Excise, the system, in its simplest form, may be illustrated as follows:

		£	£
1.	A manufacturer buys raw materials at a basic price of	1,000	
	on which his supplier charges VAT at 17½%, i.e.	175	
	giving a cost to the manufacturer of	1,175	
2.	The manufacturer sells to a wholesaler goods produced from the raw materials at a basic price of	2,000	
	to which he adds VAT of	350	
	the wholesaler paying	2,350	
3.	The manufacturer pays to the Customs and Excise VAT on his invoice	350	
	Less: VAT on his purchase	175	
	a net payment of		175
4.	The wholesaler sells the goods to a retailer at	2,800	
	plus VAT	490	
	the retailer paying	3,290	
5.	The wholesaler pays to the Customs and Excise: VAT on his invoice	490	
	Less: VAT on his purchase	350	
	a net payment of		140
6.	The retailer sells to the consumer at	4,200	
	plus VAT	735	
	the consumer paying	4,935	
7.	The retailer pays to the Customs and Excise: VAT on his sale	735	
	Less: VAT on his purchase	490	
	a net payment of		245
	The total tax to Customs is		560

This £560 represents 17½% on the value added to the raw material, i.e. 17½% of (£4,200–£1,000).

8.3 TAXABLE SUPPLIES

VAT is payable only where there is a taxable supply, i.e. the goods or services are those covered by the tax and are not exempt or zero-rated. VAT is payable on imports of taxable goods as though it were a customs duty, and it may be payable by a UK agent who is working on commission for an overseas principal.

Goods produced by a business or acquired by a business and used for the purposes of that business, e.g. stationery printed in the business, are taxable at market value. This is the process known for VAT purposes as 'self supply'. Where, however, goods are produced by a business or acquired by a business and applied by the owner for personal use, the cost of those goods is taxable. Cost is not defined for this purpose but, in the case of manufactured articles, it is thought to mean direct cost, e.g. materials and labour, plus manufacturing overheads.

Samples and promotional gifts are taxable at the cost to the supplier but if that cost is no more than £50, from 6 April 2001 (previously £15), they will be tax free. VAT can be recovered on the cost of gifts over the limit if they are accompanied by a certificate indicating that output tax will be accounted for. Industrial samples for testing and market research are also tax free, whatever their cost or value, provided they are not of the kind obtainable in the market place.

Goods supplied on hire purchase are taxable on their cash price, i.e. excluding interest or hire purchase charges, which are not subject to VAT.

Goods and services will be taxed net of cash discount, provided the rate is shown on the invoice and whether or not the discount is taken by the customer.

For retailers using the cash basis, VAT is paid on cash received, so that bad debts are automatically relieved of the tax. With the alternative basis, VAT is paid on credit sales invoiced plus cash sales.

8.4 THE TAX POINT

This is the point when liability to the tax arises, although the actual payment or repayment of tax may not be due until some months later. Basically the tax point is when the goods are despatched or made available to the customer, but the tax point may be extended to the date when the invoice is issued within 14 days of the despatch of the goods. The Commissioners are authorised to agree special arrangements as to the tax point with particular traders.

In the case of goods on sale or return, the tax point is when the goods have finally been accepted by the customer, but this date must not be more than 12 months after despatch to the customer.

In the case of goods on hire (not hire purchase or credit sale) the tax point is when each successive payment becomes due, and such point may be expressed in the agreement, or when an invoice is issued, if earlier.

For goods on hire purchase the tax point is when the goods are supplied.

8.5 ADMINISTRATION

Registration

A trader is obliged to register for VAT with the Customs and Excise where turnover exceeds £60,000 from 1 April 2005 (previously £58,000 from 31 March 2004). On registration, the trader must show on the invoices issued the tax added to the relevant charges, except in the case of retailers making cash sales; and must make normally quarterly returns, paying or reclaiming the difference between input and output tax. It could, however, be advantageous to register, even though turnover is expected to be below the limit, where input tax was likely to be less than output tax and the difference could be reclaimed. Registration can be cancelled where turnover is below the limit of £58,000 from 1 April 2005 (previously £56,000 from 31 March 2004).

However, these limits may be decreased in the future. There is currently a review of the limits; the registration limits in other EU countries are far lower than in the UK.

Records and tax invoices

All traders who are not exempt are obliged to keep records of their purchases and sales including records of the VAT applicable on those transactions. They are also obliged to keep what is called a 'tax account' in which their total liabilities or claims in respect of VAT are recorded. No particular form of record or account is specified. The authorities have the right to inspect records (including computer operations) and tax invoices and may obtain the power to enter premises for this purpose. Special regulations apply to the records of retailers.

All non-exempt traders, except retailers making cash sales, must issue what are called 'tax invoices' on making sales. A tax invoice is simply an ordinary invoice which contains certain specified information, i.e. the usual invoice details plus: the number of the invoice, the registered number of the supplier, the type of supply (e.g. whether zero-rated, etc.) and the tax charged. Exempt and zero-rated supplies must be separated even though they are included in one invoice with taxable goods. Invoices need not be issued for zero-rated supplies, second-hand goods relieved of tax, gifts, and goods for which input tax is not deducted.

Returns and payments

Returns showing the input and output tax for the period must normally be submitted to the Customs and Excise at specified three-monthly intervals, and these claims will show the amount of tax to be paid or repaid. Where the business is likely to obtain a repayment, application may be made for the returns and the settlement to be made monthly, thus helping to improve the cash flow of the business. From 1

April 2004, businesses with a turnover below £666,000 (previously £600,000) can opt for annual accounting subject to nine estimated payments in advance, with a tenth adjusting payment.

If returns are not made or they are inaccurate, the authorities may make an estimated assessment on the trader. Such an assessment must be made within six years after the end of the accounting period concerned but cannot be made after three years from the death of the trader. The trader may appeal against an assessment to the Commissioners and thence to a quasi-judicial body, independent of the Commissioners, known as a VAT tribunal.

Flat rate scheme for smaller businesses

The flat rate scheme is intended to be a simplification measure that allows businesses to calculate their net tax due by applying a flat rate percentage to their inclusive total turnover (i.e. including all reduced, zero-rated and exempt income). The scheme applies to certain trade sectors only. The 2003 Budget included provisions to extend the table of trade sectors to include 'mining and quarrying', 'journalism' and 'hair dressing or other beauty treatment services', with effect from 1 May 2003.

The scheme is open to small businesses with an annual taxable income (excluding VAT) not exceeding £150,000 and total turnover (including the value of exempt and non-taxable income but not including VAT) not exceeding £187,500 per year.

Penalties

Penalties, fines and interest may be payable for failure to comply with the VAT legislation. In the case of failure to pay the amount due the authorities have the ultimate power of obtaining a distress warrant with a view to the sale of the taxpayer's goods, furniture and other chattels. From 11 March 1992 a penalty will not normally be imposed unless the net VAT under-declared or overpaid exceeds £2,000 in an accounting period.

Serious misdeclarations are those where on one return 30% of the tax managed (input and output) is under-declared; or more than £1 million. From 11 March 1992 the penalty in such cases was reduced from 20% to 15% and a period of grace is normally given if the misdeclaration is rectified in the next return. A default surcharge applies to late returns and late payments on three occasions, the maximum penalty being 15%. Reliefs are available for small businesses with annual turnover of less than £150,000 in relation to the penalties for late payment of tax.

Cash accounting

Registered persons must inform the Customs and Excise for VAT to be based on the amounts paid and received during a quarterly or monthly accounting period. This system can simplify the accounting requirements for many of the smaller businesses and, where substantial credit is given to customers, improve the cash flow. Bad debts are automatically accounted for by failure to receive the amount due.

Two significant changes to the rules for reclaiming VAT on bad debts were included in the Finance Act 2002.

- A business claiming bad debt relief is no longer required to send a written notice to the debtor.
- A business that has claimed input tax on a supply but has not paid the supplier within six months of the supply (or payment due date, if later) must repay the input tax to Customs and Excise.

It could be a disadvantage in terms of cash flow when tax receivable on purchases is higher than tax payable on sales and where long terms of credit are taken on supplies.

Cash accounting is available where turnover is not expected to exceed £666,000 in the year from 1 April 2004 (previously £600,000), and can continue until turnover reaches £825,000. The VAT outstanding must not exceed £5,000. It operates from the beginning of the normal tax period for the business and must be continued for at least two years. Transactions excluded from a cash accounting system are: imports, exports, hire purchase, conditional and credit sales.

Tax invoices must continue to be kept and, for cash (not cheque) payments, they need to be receipted. Receipts and payments by credit card are entered at the date of the invoice, but giro transactions, standing orders and direct debits at the date of entry in the bank account. Part payments or receipts should be related to specific invoices.

8.6 EXEMPT TRADERS

These are (a) small traders with a turnover of no more than £60,000 from 1 April 2005 (previously £58,000 from 1 April 2004), and (b) traders who deal only with exempt supplies. The first category need not register, do not have to charge VAT on their sales, and are not liable to account for VAT, but they cannot recover from the Customs and Excise the VAT charged on their purchases. They can register voluntarily and if they do so they are no longer exempt. The second category of trader cannot obtain refunds of input tax, but where there are both taxable and exempt supplies a proportion of the input tax is refundable.

8.7 EXEMPT GOODS AND SERVICES

A large number of kinds of goods and services are exempt from VAT – that is to say, VAT cannot be charged when such goods are sold, even by a registered trader. These categories are summarised below.

Group 1 The grant of any interest in or right over land but not the letting of accommodation, parking or camping facilities or fishing or taking game. Bedroom accommodation in hotels is taxable but not other accommodation in hotels, or elsewhere. From 1 August 1989 an election (subject to many qualifications) can be made to waive this exemption, and thus recover input tax.

Group 2 Insurance, covering also services provided by brokers and agents; but most marine, aviation and transport insurance is zero-rated. Note that insurance premium tax was imposed from 1 October 1994 (currently 5%).

Group 3 Postal services, but not cable services.

Group 4 Betting, gaming and lotteries, but admission charges, club subscriptions and takings from gaming machines are taxable.

Group 5 Finance, i.e. dealing in money or credit, banking and the sale of securities, but stockbrokers' commissions and unit trust management fees are taxable. The charge made by credit card companies on retailers is exempt. where banks buy in credit card processing, the charge for this service will no longer be exempt from 9 March 1999 (Budget Day).

Group 6 Education, including the supply of incidental services and covering the facilities provided by youth clubs and similar organisations.

Group 7 Health, covering goods and services provided by medical practitioners, dentists, opticians (the eye test is exempt, as is carrying out the resulting prescription, but the provision of spectacles is not (from 1 July 2001, VAT @ 17.5% will be charged on the total cost)), nurses, pharmaceutical chemists, hearing aid dispensers, hospitals, etc. Protective boots and helmets purchased by businesses are chargeable from 1 April 1989.

Group 8 Burial and cremation services.

Group 9 Trade unions and professional bodies.

Group 10 Sports competitions and physical education.

Group 11 Works of art, etc. Disposals exempt from capital gains tax. (See also under Section 8.9.)

Group 12 Fundraising by charities.

Group 13 Cultural services, etc.

8.8 ZERO-RATED SUPPLIES

Zero-rating means that, although the goods are theoretically taxable, the rate of tax is nil. Because zero-rated goods are taxable, suppliers of these goods can recover tax they have suffered on relevant purchases; they do not, however, charge tax on their sales of zero-rated goods. All goods exported by a registered trader are zero-rated, but not in 1985/86 and onwards goods exported or imported for processing and re-exported. Other zero-rated supplies are set out in Schedule 8 VAT Act 1994, subsequent statutory orders, and the Finance Act 1989, and these groups are summarised below.

Group 1 Food for human consumption, including many packaged goods, animal feeding stuffs, but not soft drinks (it has now been held that freshly-pressed citrus fruits are zero-rated), alcoholic drinks, confectionery, ice-cream, petfoods, seeds, and animals yielding food for human consumption. There are many exemptions to the above.

Group 2 Water, other than distilled water, and sewerage services except when supplied to businesses from 1 July 1990.

Group 3 Publications such as books, newspapers, periodicals, music, maps, etc., but not stationery.

Group 4 Talking books, radio sets, boats, maintenance of 'talking books', recorders and magnetic tape and radio sets for use by the blind and handicapped. From 1 April 1986 much other equipment for handicapped persons or charities was zero-rated, including lifts, alarms and welfare vehicles; from 1 April 1989 medical sterilising equipment for charities; and from 1 April 1992 toilet facilities in charitable buildings.

Group 5 Construction of dwellings, residential accommodation and charitable purposes and the grant of a major interest in the property, including sale of the freehold or grant of lease for over 21 years, but only when the trader is the person constructing the building. Residential accommodation includes homes for children, the aged and infirm, students, the armed forces, monasteries and nunneries. In accordance with EU law the construction of new industrial and commercial buildings will be subject to VAT for contracts made after 1 April 1989. The letting for one or two weeks in a year of time-share holiday homes by a long lease is not zero-rated (Cottage Holiday Assoc. Ltd. v Customs and

Excise, 1982). Note that land is exempt and that the maintenance of buildings is chargeable at the VAT rate. From 1 June 1984 VAT applies to structural alterations, sheds and greenhouses in private gardens, and fixtures in new buildings, but not to substantial conversion, alteration and enlargement of ancient monuments and listed buildings. From 1 April 1986 zero-rating applied to building alterations for the benefit of a resident handicapped person.

Landlords can opt to charge VAT on non-residential rents from 1 August 1989. In this case tenants pay tax on half the rents in the first year, or for five years where they are charities.

Group 6 Protected buildings.

Group 7 Services to overseas traders or for overseas purposes.

Group 8 Transport, covering the supply, services and maintenance of ships above 15 tons and not used for recreational purposes; and aircraft above 18,000 pounds and not used for recreation; and the transport of passengers in vehicles carrying 12 or more passengers (i.e. excluding taxis). Airline meals are not taxable.

Group 9 Caravans above the limits for use as trailers (i.e. 22.9 feet in length or 7.5 feet in width) and houseboats.

Group 10 Gold bullion and gold coins, when supplied by a Central Bank to another Central Bank or to and from a Central Bank to a member of the London Gold Market. The Finance Act 1993 s45 provides that on and after 1 April 1993 where any person makes a supply of gold for business purposes that supply is a taxable supply, but not a zero-rated supply. Where the supplier is a taxable person and the supplies are made in connection with the business of the customer, the latter (i.e. the purchaser) must account for and pay tax on the supply on the supplier's behalf. The supplies may consist of gold, gold coins and goods containing gold, taxable at the open market value of the gold contained in the goods.

Group 11 Bank notes.

Group 12 Drugs, medicines and appliances supplied on prescription, whether under the National Health Service or otherwise including from 10 March 1981 ambulances and wheelchairs supplied to hospitals and car adaptations for the disabled; also in 1984/85 and onwards cars leased to disabled persons under mobility schemes; in 1985/86 medical and scientific equipment, including computers, donated to hospitals; in 1986/87 bathroom equipment for the handicapped in charitable residential homes, and equipment for charitable first aid and rescue services.

Group 13 Imports and exports subject to qualifications.

Group 14 Tax-free shops

Group 15 Charities. Much equipment used or supplied by charities is zero-rated (see also under Group 4) and zero-rating is applied to medicinal products supplied to a charity for medical research, both for humans and animals – see Value Added Tax (Handicapped Persons and Charities Order) 1986. Also, from 1 April 1991 television, radio and cinema advertising, donated goods, and equipment for veterinary research.

Group 16 Clothing for young children, industrial safety clothing and motor cycle crash helmets.

Also zero-rated from 1 April 1993 are protective boots and helmets and parts and equipment for certain ships and aircraft not used for recreation.

8.9 THE LOWER 5% RATE

VAT on domestic fuel was reduced to 5% in 1997. The subsequent Finance Acts have extended the 5% band to include:

(a) Domestic energy-saving materials – the supply and installation of energy-saving materials such as insulation, draught stripping, hot water and central heating system controls, as well as solar panels, to all homes. This was introduced from 1 April 2000 but does not apply to the DIY market. However, from 1 June 2002, the 5% VAT rate will apply to the domestic installation of grant-funded heating equipment.

(b) Women's sanitary products (from 1 January 2001).

(c) Children's car seats from (11 May 2000).

(d) Certain residential conversions and renovation of dwellings (from 11 May 2000).

(e) Air source heat pumps and micro combined heat and power units (from 7 April 2005)

(f) Supplies of advice or information relating to the welfare of the elderly or disabled, and children.

8.10 MISCELLANEOUS

- **Business entertainment**. Tax suffered on business entertaining cannot be deducted from output tax. Tax on allowable subsistence for business purposes is, however, deductible from output tax.

- **Hotel accommodation, catering and tourism**. Up to four weeks accommodation, including board and service, is taxable at the current VAT rate. After four weeks, the charge for the rent of the room or rooms is not taxable. The charge for the use of services will be assumed to be not less than 20% of the accommodation charge excluding meals. The charge for meals will also bear the current rate. Gross profits by tour operators on tours in the European Union are taxable.

- **Second-hand Goods**. From 1 January 1995 the margin scheme of VAT applies to all second-hand goods, works of art, antiques and collectors' items but not to precious metals and gem stones.

8.11 MOTOR CARS

VAT

VAT is charged by the seller on the price charged to the buyer and is reclaimable by a dealer whose business it is to sell cars, and by companies buying their own cars wholly for business use (from 1 August 1995).

Reclaiming VAT

An individual or company buying a car for use in the business, or for private use, cannot reclaim the tax which it has paid to the dealer or on importing the car, unless it is acquired new for re-sale or for use in, or lease to, taxi firms, self-drive hire firms and driving schools, subject to adjustment for personal use.

Vehicles chargeable to VAT

These are essentially private type cars for use on public roads and constructed or adapted for carrying passengers. Vehicles not chargeable are those accommodating only one, or more than twelve, passengers; of above 3 tonnes unladen weight; caravans, ambulances, prison vans, approved taxi cabs; and special vehicles not for carrying passengers, such as ice-cream vans, mobile shops and offices, hearses and bullion vans. VAT is payable when an exempt vehicle is converted to carry passengers. Cars used by manufacturers for research and development are relieved from VAT from 1 April 1989. From 29 July 1989 exemption was extended to cars leased to handicapped persons, and to members of visiting forces and to individuals with diplomatic privileges.

Leasing and hire purchase

VAT must be paid on the sale price when a car is acquired by hire purchase and can be reclaimed by a dealer. If a car is leased VAT must be charged on the rentals and can be reclaimed by the lessor if in business, but only 50% where any use of the car is made for private motoring. Vehicles purchased for leasing to the disabled are relieved from car tax from 1 April 1989. (See also under 'Reclaiming VAT' above.) No refunds of VAT can be claimed where businesses buy company cars on long leases from EU suppliers who do not conduct business in the UK.

Repairs and maintenance

VAT is chargeable on the cost and can be reclaimed in full by a business even if there is some private use.

Sale of used cars

Basically VAT must be charged on the sale price of used cars, whether sold by a dealer or by a business using the car for the business. However, the special scheme applicable to such sales enables the VAT to be charged only on the excess of the selling price over the purchase price of the car. No tax invoice is issued and the input tax cannot be reclaimed.

Fuel benefit

This is the scale charge for income tax on fuel provided free or below cost to employees for their private mileage.

Car fuel scale rates

The following reduced scale charges will apply from the start of the first VAT return period beginning on or after 1 May 2005.

Annual returns

Cylinder capacity of vehicle	Scale charge diesel £	VAT due per car £	Scale charge petrol £	VAT due car £
Up to 1,400 cc	945.00	140.74	985.00	146.70
1,401 cc to 2,000 cc	945.00	140.74	1,245.00	185.43
2,001 cc or more	1,200.00	178.72	1,830.00	272.55

Quarterly returns

Cylinder capacity of vehicle	Scale charge diesel £	VAT due per car £	Scale charge petrol £	VAT due car £
Up to 1,400 cc	236.00	35.15	246.00	36.64
1,401 cc to 2,000 cc	236.00	35.15	311.00	46.32
2,001 cc or more	300.00	44.68	457.00	68.06

Monthly returns

Cylinder capacity of vehicle	Scale charge diesel £	VAT due per car £	Scale charge petrol £	VAT due car £
Up to 1,400 cc	78.00	11.62	82.00	12.21
1,401 cc to 2,000 cc	78.00	11.62	103.00	15.34
2,001 cc or more	100.00	14.89	152.00	22.64

Where VAT is reclaimed on fuel used for private purposes VAT according to scale is added to the output tax. It may not be beneficial to reclaim VAT on fuel if the amount so claimed is less than the scale charge.

8.12 RETAILERS

Retailers are not obliged to prepare tax invoices unless they are demanded by customers, and hence a number of special schemes for accounting for VAT are available for retailers and are set out in Notice 727 issued by the Customs and Excise.

8.13 BAD DEBTS

Normally, where a supplier has suffered a bad debt incurred by an insolvent customer, the supplier can reclaim VAT he has already paid on the supplies concerned. The sale must have been at open-market value and the property in the goods must have passed. The supplier must prove in the bankruptcy, or liquidation in the case of a limited company, for the debt less the VAT.

As mentioned above (Section 8.5 Administration – Cash accounting) two significant changes to the rules for reclaiming VAT on bad debts were introduced in the Finance Act 2002.

- A business claiming bad debt relief can no longer be required to send a written notice to the debtor.
- A business that has claimed input tax on a supply but has not paid the

supplier within six months of the supply (or payment due date, if later) must repay the input tax to Customs and Excise.

By the exercise of an option for cash accounting, where turnover is below £666,000, bad debts will be automatically relieved from VAT. From 1 April 1993 VAT can be reclaimed on bad debts which are more than six months old based on date of supply (previously one year old) and have been written off in the trader's accounts; from 6 October 1997 relief for bad debts is available for barter transactions; the relief can be back-dated to when the debt arose. A three-year limit is to be put on the age of the bad debt.

8.14 DIRECTORS' ACCOMMODATION

VAT is not recoverable on costs, such as repairs, incurred on accommodation provided by companies for directors or their families.

8.15 TREATMENT FOR INCOME AND CORPORATION TAX

Persons exempt from VAT

Allowable business expenses can include VAT charged on purchases, etc.

Other persons

Income and expenditure is to be brought into the tax computation exclusive of VAT.

8.16 SINGLE EUROPEAN MARKET

From 1 January 1993, border controls between members of the European Union (EU) are largely abolished.

Before 1 January 1993 controls of imports and exports were carried out by Customs and Exercise at the frontiers. As a result the exporter had to claim customs clearance for zero-rating on the shipment of goods and for imports before the goods were released by customs.

From 1 January 1993 VAT is charged, if applicable, not on the importation of goods but on the acquisition from other EU states. The tax point of 'acquisition' is the 15th of the month following acquisition, or the date of the invoice. Where goods pass from an EU state to a non-EU state, controls at the border will remain. To obtain zero-rating of exports, the supplier must show on his invoice not only his UK VAT registration number but also that of his customer in the importing state, and submit to the Customs a quarterly list of such exports.

Where customers are not VAT-registered sales up to various limits (depending on the EU state concerned) are chargeable to VAT. Above these limits VAT is payable in the importing state and this may involve appointing a VAT representative in that state.

The members of the EU, with effect from 1 May 2004, are the UK, Austria, Finland, Sweden, Germany, France, Italy, Spain, Belgium, Portugal, Denmark, Greece, Ireland, Luxembourg, the Netherlands, Cyprus*, Czech Republic, Estonia, Hungary, Latvia, Lithuania, Malta, Poland, Slovakia and Slovenia.

The European Commission has advised that, although the entire island of Cyprus joined the EU on 1 May 2004, the application of EU law will be suspended in those areas of Cyprus in which the Government of the Republic of Cyprus does not exercise effective control.

9

Inheritance Tax

9.1 GENERAL NATURE OF THE TAX

Inheritance Tax may arise on the amount of a taxpayer's wealth passing on death, on certain lifetime transfers and on certain transfers into and out of trusts. The tax applies when the total value of the estate and the chargeable transfers exceeds £275,000 in 2005/06 (£263,000 in 2004/05) for deaths and the rate is 40%. Subject to the many exemptions indicated below, the amount chargeable to the tax includes the value of property both in and outside the UK where the deceased was domiciled in the UK; but only property in the UK is valued for those domiciled elsewhere, although in such cases double taxation relief may apply.

The Finance Act 1986 gave the new title of 'inheritance tax' to what was previously called 'capital transfer tax'. The latter tax was not repealed but was substantially amended, particularly by the elimination of tax on most lifetime gifts. The amended provisions apply to deaths after 17 March 1986 and gifts or transfers made after that date.

The following sections cover only the essentials of inheritance tax, which represents a very complex body of legislation. For more detailed information it will be necessary to obtain expert professional advice.

9.2 EXEMPTIONS

- Property passing on death and seven years before death up to a value of £275,000 in 2005/06 (£263,000 in 2004/05).

- Transfers or gifts between husband and wife made on death or at any time previously, subject to a limit of £55,000 if the recipient is domiciled abroad.

- Gifts which represent normal expenditure out of income.

- Lifetime gifts in consideration of (i.e. before) marriage: those by the parents of the married couple up to £5,000; by a remoter ancestor up to £2,500; and by others up to £1,000.

- Gifts to charities, for national purposes and the national benefit; also gifts to political parties.

- Cash options to widows and dependents under approved annuity schemes and certain overseas pensions.

- Tax-free government securities in the beneficial ownership of persons not domiciled or ordinarily resident in the UK; and all property outside the UK owned by such persons.

- Gifts for the maintenance or education of a spouse, child or dependant.

- Majority holdings of shares given to employees on trust.

- Legacies disclaimed within two years of death.

- Lifetime transfers up to £3,000 a year, this limit excluding the small gifts exemption of £250 a year.

- Bona fide transfers of property in the course of trade for adequate consideration and allowable for income tax.

- Where death was attributable to injury or disease arising from active service with the armed forces.

9.3 THE VALUE TRANSFERRED

Where a specific sum of money is given, either on death or during lifetime, the value transferred is the amount of money in question. In the case of transfers of other assets, such as investments, jewellery, furniture, land and buildings, the asset will need to be valued at market value at the date of transfer. More strictly the value to be taken into account is the loss in value to the donor.

Transfers of shares in unquoted companies made within seven years before death (except to a wife) should be made at a freely negotiated price, so that no chargeable benefit arises.

The gross value of the estate at death may include interests in applicable trusts, such as discretionary trusts and sums due to the estate, such as under life policies and death benefit under pensions schemes. From the gross value of the estate deductions are made for debts, including income tax due at death, and funeral expenses, but not executorship expenses.

Other lifetime transfers which are not potentially exempt transfers (see below) are chargeable at half the full rate. Where death occurs within 7 years the balance of the full rate becomes payable, subject to tapering relief (see below).

9.4 GIFTS WITHIN SEVEN YEARS OF DEATH

Up to 17 March 1986 chargeable gifts and transfers made within 10 years of death were chargeable to tax at the lifetime rate of capital transfer tax. Gifts made after 17 March 1986 within seven years of death will be chargeable to the appropriate rate of inheritance tax, subject to 'tapering relief' – see below.

9.5 TAPERING RELIEF

The tax payable on chargeable gifts or transfers made within three to seven years of death is reduced or 'tapered' according to the following scale:

Period before death	Proportion of tax rate payable
6 to 7 years	20%
5 to 6 years	40%
4 to 5 years	60%
3 to 4 years	80%
up to 3 years	full rate

9.6 POTENTIALLY EXEMPT TRANSFERS (PET)

These are transfers which will only become chargeable if death occurs within seven years after they are made. They include gifts to individuals and accumulation and maintenance trusts set up for members of the deceased's family or for the disabled. They do not include transfers into discretionary settlements which are chargeable lifetime transfers.

Where a PET becomes a chargeable transfer because of death, the tax payable on it is determined by any gifts made in the 7 years prior to that gift. This means that any gift made in the 14 years before death will either incur a direct liability (within 7 years of death) or increase the liability on a gift inside the 7-year period (if such a gift is made within 7 years of the first gift).

9.7 GIFTS WITH RESERVATIONS

These are gifts made after 17 March 1986 with a reservation for the donor to obtain a benefit. Examples of reservations would be the retention of a right to obtain income or enjoy the gifted property, to continue to live in a gifted house, inheritance trusts and insurance policies for the mitigation of the tax.

A gift with reservations to an individual will be taxed on the death of the donor, but one made to a trust or company will be taxed when it is made. Tax will be charged on the gift when the reservation is released, or the enjoyment of the property ceases, e.g. on the death of the donor, subject to credit for any tax already paid. Exceptions include the case where reasonable provision is made for a relative who becomes unable to maintain himself or herself after the gift was made.

Pre-owned Assets Tax

The Government introduced a new income tax by way of the Finance Act 2004. The charge is intended to apply where arrangements have been made which save

Inheritance Tax by which a person gives away assets but continues to use or enjoy those assets.

Broadly, pre-owned assets are assets which were at one time owned by a chargeable person but which have been disposed of wholly or in part since March 1986. The legislation has introduced separate rules which set out what counts as enjoyment of assets and how to calculate the tax charge in respect of land, items of personal property and intangible assets (for example, shares or insurance policies).

The tax comes into effect from 6 April 2005 but it is important to understand that it will be imposed in respect of schemes or arrangements set up before the tax was announced - back as far as March 1986.

Where the tax applies, it will be charged as if the chargeable person's income was increased by the deemed value of the benefit received. For example, if the asset given away was property with a market rental value of £25,000 per annum, then the chargeable person would be treated as though his income was increased by £25,000 and he will be taxed at his highest marginal rates, even though he has not received any such income.

There are some exemptions built into the legislation and tax-payers can opt, if they wish to avoid the tax, to accept that the assets given away will be treated as if they still form part of their estate for Inheritance Tax purposes only.

9.8 OTHER RELIEFS

The more important other reliefs are as follows:

Business Property Relief

Where a transfer of value includes relevant business property, the value transferred is reduced by a percentage (currently either 100% or 50%). This is known as business property relief (BPR).

BPR does not have to be claimed, it is given automatically. It is given in respect of lifetime tax, death tax and tax on trusts.

For transfers on and after 10 March 1992 and any recalculation of tax on earlier transfers following a death on or after that date, the relief is given at the following rates.

Relevant business property	Percentage 10.3.92 to 5.4.96	Reduction 6.4.96 to present
A business carried on by a sole trader	100%	100%
An interest in a business, e.g. partnership	100%	100%

Transfer out of shares in or securities of a company which are listed and held by a controlling shareholder	50%	50%
Transfer out of shares in or securities of a company which are not listed and held by a controlling shareholder	100%	100%
Transfer out of a substantial minority shareholding (i.e. >25%) in an unlisted company	50%	100%
Land, buildings, machinery or plant owned by an individual and used by a company, partnership he controls	50%	100%
Land, buildings, machinery or plant owned by a settlement	50% or 100% *	50% or 100%*

* Assets held by a trust can only qualify for BPR if:

(a) they are used for the purposes of a business carried on by a person with an interest in possession in the trust that owns the assets; and

(b) that business comprises relevant business property.

100% BPR is available on the transfer of the trust assets if the business in which those assets are used is transferred at the same time. Only 50% BPR is available in situations where there is a transfer of trust assets but the business itself is not transferred but retained by the person with the interest in possession.

An interest in possession in settled property exists where the person having the interest has an immediate entitlement to any income produced by that property as the income arises.

Agricultural land

100% relief from inheritance tax is available, subject to conditions, for agricultural land passing after 10 March 1992 (previously 50%). The main conditions are:

● That the property was occupied by the deceased (or transferor) for the purpose of agriculture throughout the period of two years before death or transfer;

● That the property was owned by the deceased (or transferor) for seven years before death (or transfer) and occupied for that purpose by the deceased (or transferor) or by another person;

● The relief applies to leases of agricultural land at full market value; from 28 November 1995 relief is available for farmland subject to agricultural tenancies acquired as a result of the death of the previous tenant. The death must have occurred on or after 1 September 1995.

- In all other cases the relief is at 50%.

- The 1996 Budget introduced relief for land dedicated to wildlife habitats.

Quick succession relief

This is a scaled reduction of the tax payable on death where the deceased received chargeable transfers within five years before death. The tax is reduced by 80% where the transfer was made two years before death, 60% for three years, 40% for four years and 20% for five years.

Property sales

Where sales are made on or after 10 March 1993 of freehold or leasehold property, and the sale is made within 4 years after death (previously 3 years), the sale price may be substituted for the value at death for inheritance tax purposes.

9.9 RE-ARRANGEMENT OF ESTATES

Within two years after death the dispositions of an estate made by a will can be rearranged by the written agreement of all beneficiaries, and this could have the effect of reducing inheritance tax. In 1989/90 and onwards these rearrangements will only be effective for inheritance tax purposes where they make adequate provision for the dependents of the deceased.

9.10 GENERAL CONCLUSIONS

The foregoing is no more than a résumé of the essentials of this highly complex tax. Expert professional advice is of the greatest importance when taxpayers seek to mitigate this tax. Subject to proper advice, the tax can be relieved by such methods as: taking advantage of the annual exemptions for gifts, transfers to spouses and to charities, and the establishment of trusts for children and dependents. If the risk of dying within seven years is accepted, substantial gifts during lifetime instead of legacies at death may be appropriate.

Notes to readers

Index

GEORGE VYNER LTD.,
PO Box 1,
Holmfirth,
HD9 7YP
Tel. 01484-685221
Fax. 01484-688538

Simplified Book-keeping for Small Businesses

by Geoffrey Whitehead   **£7.99**

A book specially designed, incorporating
Vyner's 'Simplex' system of account books,
to assist the small trader in keeping adequate accounts.

Simplex Account Books:

Simplex D Account Book	£12.14
Simplex VAT Record Book	£14.21
Simplex Licensees and Caterers Account Book	£16.64
Simplex Wages Book	£8.69
Simplex Farm Account Book	£16.64
Simplex No. 2 Parcel Post Book	£4.65
Simplex Mileage Record Book	£3.99

The price of Simplex account books includes VAT.
Please enclose £1.75 per title for postage.

Standing Order for

TAXATION SIMPLIFIED

To: Management Books 2000 Ltd
Forge House, Limes Road
Kemble
Cirencester
Gloucestershire GL7 6AD
tel: 01285 771441
fax: 01285 771055
email: info@mb2000.com

Please forward me a copy of TAXATION SIMPLIFIED together with an invoice on publication until further notice, starting with the 2006/07 edition, due in Spring 2006

Name _____

Address

_____
_____
_____
_____ postcode _____
Telephone _____

Signature _____

Please photocopy this page to avoid damaging your book

TS 2005/06

Advantage of joining the subscription list – we offer the current edition
(next one will be Taxation Simplified 2006/07) at £1 off the cover price
and no post and packing to our subscribers. TIME TO JOIN THE LIST!
Copy and post this form straight away.